FROM DISSERTATI

Chicago Guides
to Writing, Editing,
and Publishing

WILLIAM GERMANO

FROM
DISSERTATION
TO BOOK

THE UNIVERSITY OF CHICAGO PRESS
CHICAGO AND LONDON

William Germano is vice president and publishing director
at Routledge. Previously he served as humanities editor
and editorial director at Columbia University Press. His
Getting It Published (2001) was also published by
the University of Chicago Press.

The University of Chicago Press, Chicago 60637
The University of Chicago Press, Ltd., London
© 2005 by William Germano
All rights reserved. Published 2005
Printed in the United States of America
14 13 12 11 10 09 08 07 06 05   1 2 3 4 5
ISBN: 0-226-28845-5 (cloth)
ISBN: 0-226-28846-3 (paper)

Library of Congress Cataloging-in-Publication Data

Germano, William P.
  From dissertation to book / William Germano.
    p. cm. — (Chicago guides to writing, editing, and
    publishing)
  Includes bibliographical references and index.
  ISBN 0-226-28845-5 (cloth : alk. paper) —
  ISBN 0-226-28846-3 (pbk. : alk. paper)
  1. Editing. 2. Authorship—Marketing. 3. Academic
  writing. I. Title. II. Series.
PN162.G37 2005
808'.02—dc22   2004019345

♾ The paper used in this publication meets the minimum
requirements of the American National Standard for
Information Sciences—Permanence of Paper for Printed
Library Materials, ANSI Z39.48-1992.

For Bill Regier

CONTENTS

ACKNOWLEDGMENTS

On the Road. Many people have given generously of their time to talk with me about what a doctoral dissertation is and what it might mean to revise one. Again and again I have been reminded that there are brilliant, committed scholars and teachers everywhere, and not only at the major research institutions.

I am particularly grateful for the opportunity to test-drive some of what follows in these pages with faculty and graduate students at universities and academic meetings across the United States and Canada. Caught between the dilemma of thanking many hosts by name or asking them to lip-read my gratitude, I'll choose, at least this time, the latter route. I thank them here for the chance to learn and to teach.

Shop Talk. Of my publishing friends, colleagues, and authors, I can only repeat that from them I learn daily what books must be in order to survive. Some of those publishing professionals read early drafts, and like the University of Chicago Press's anonymous readers, saved me from driving onto the shoulder. It is a pleasure once again to work with the excellent staff of the Press, including my manuscript editor, Carol Saller. My editor, Linda Halvorson, runs the Press's imposing reference division, and still managed to make me feel that this little manuscript was of particular importance to her and to the house. She insisted that my book make sense. My agent, Tanya McKinnon, insisted that I get it done. I thank them, too.

At the Blackboard. A special note of appreciation to the students in my book editing class at NYU's Publishing Program; a semester of their questions helped me work out some of the ideas in this book.

Home. This project found its shape on the same kitchen table where Diane Gibbons and I wrote doctoral dissertations, the hard way—with a typewriter. Our son Christian tolerated the creation of this book with all the equanimity a twelve-year-old can supply. Thanks would hardly be enough.

1

Why This Book

The morning after defending the doctoral thesis is the first day of a scholar's brave new world. But aside from recommending that you publish, graduate schools rarely take the time to explain just what you should *do* with your dissertation. There's an expectation that the student is on the brink, or that this excellent piece of new scholarship will naturally find its place in the academic firmament. But how to get it there? And in what form?

Senior professors are often too far from the process to give useful advice. Junior faculty are usually just as puzzled as graduate students by the mechanics of scholarly publication. But each year, many dissertations are written, and some are published. Among those, a few become widely read works that transform not only what but how we think.

To the new Ph.D.'s eager question—"What do I do now that I'm done?"—this book offers answers rather than *an* answer. There can't be just one. The key to any of them, though, is revision.

Revision can mean a lot of different things, maybe especially for scholars. Young academics talk about revising their dissertations when they mean they will do hardly anything at all, or rewrite every sentence, or settle for something in between. This book is in part about what can be done with a doctoral dissertation, choosing among your options, and moving forward. Wherever you begin, and whatever investment of time and energy you plan to make, your goal is to take something already written and make it more.

Taking that dissertation and making it "more" isn't a

straight path. It's a curving route with loops and off-ramps. Yet once you know where you want to go, there are more and less efficient ways of getting there. *From Dissertation to Book* is itself meant to be a map, charting out your possibilities and giving you driving instructions.

Over the past twenty-five years, I've seen hundreds of books through to publication. As any editor knows, you whittle down thousands of proposals to get to those chosen hundreds. My job has also given me the chance to work with other editors on books they were considering for publication. Sometimes I have learned most from reviewing a thick stack of proposals other editors were keen to put forward. This part of my job is editing from ten thousand feet up. I've got a few minutes to study how an editor presents a rationale, a marketing strategy, and a financial analysis, as well as what our reviewers have to say, and what the author's own words tell about clarity and purpose. In ways I could hardly articulate, this book is a product of my engagements with all of those manuscripts and proposals.

Publishers and academic authors view books in ways that overlap, but that are hardly identical. Academics, like all writers, think that a great book idea is its own justification. Publishers want something that can stand as a book, not just a good idea indifferently presented. That means getting some key things right—shape, length, voice—so that the audience the author believes is out there will want the result enough to buy it.

It can be a shock to hear that your wonderful thesis now needs to be entirely rethought. A young scholar's writing life begins with an apparent contradiction: a dissertation needs to be written, yet no publisher has to want it when it's done. I meet a lot of scholars frustrated that academic publishers seem to brush off what graduate schools oblige their students to produce. But scholarly publishers look for at least two things in a proposal beyond a great idea and dandy prose. One is the author's credentials—how an academic's training and appointment enabled him or her to write the book in the first place. The second is what we call the author's platform. By that we mean the reputation and visibility the author has already established, and how, acting together, they will help get the intended book to its audience. You don't have much of a platform coming straight out of graduate school, but during a career of writing and publishing and lecturing, you can build a wider base and on it build broader ideas for broader audiences. Revising your dissertation, as unglamorous an activity as it may be, is the first step in creating a structure to climb.

Scholars know that our appetite for knowledge, right alongside our ignorance, grows daily. But what we call "the market" has undergone radical changes, making access to ideas increasingly challenging. Libraries buy books ever more cautiously. Readers looking for answers or information prefer a short ride on a search engine to the slower and more complex demands of a book. Independent bookstores, once a haven for scholarly works, are endangered treasures. Neither campus stores nor the chain giants (often the same thing) can provide all that the academic community would like to see on the shelf. It's much harder for a scholarly book to be published today than it was thirty years ago.

Faculty members now approaching retirement came of age when it was possible to have highly specialized work published by a leading university press. These days, young scholars are often thinking about the second book *before tenure*—even though there are senior faculty in their departments who were tenured on a handful of articles and never went on to write a book at all. Buddhist calm might be the best response to this inequity; bitterness and resentment certainly won't help. The best advice I can offer is to be pragmatic: take your own strengths and make them stronger.

These are hard times for scholars and their publishers. Yet even in hard times, it's important to remember that many dissertations can become manuscripts strong enough to be considered for publication, and a good number of them can become books. It's possible to revise a dissertation and to turn it into something more, but to do this well means first taking stock of what one has and what it might become. Turning a dissertation into a book manuscript is one option facing the recent Ph.D.; it isn't the only one, though. A dissertation can become many things—a single scholarly article, a handful of them, a specialized monograph, a broader scholarly work, a trade book, even the seeds of two or more distinct projects that could occupy the author for decades.

Some dissertations *do* get turned into books. Martin Jay's *Dialectical Imagination* and Kate Millett's *Sexual Politics* began as doctoral theses. So did Daniel Goldhagen's *Hitler's Willing Executioners,* Mitchell Duneier's *Slim's Table,* and Jill Lepore's *The Name of War.* Major works published each year began as doctoral dissertations. However much publishers may complain about the surfeit of Ph.D. theses, however much editors may say they rarely consider them, there are always hunter-gatherers at scholarly houses who want the exceptional dissertation. Some editors track dissertation abstracts. Others pay particular attention to award-winning dissertations in their fields. Still others rely on their most trusted faculty advisors to slip them advance information on the very best dissertations being written in the discipline. If you have written an outstanding doctoral thesis, chances are very good that at least one publisher would like to talk to you about it.

But what makes a dissertation outstanding to a publisher isn't exactly the same thing that makes it outstanding to the scholarly community. The winner of the prize for the year's outstanding thesis in the field of Kwakiutl grammar may have made a signal contribution to the study of linguistics. A publisher, however, will see the prize only as a validation of the dissertation's academic quality. That might be enough to get a foot in the door. An outstanding book would be something more, as well as something different. Perhaps the author has explained a feature of this language in such a way that those of us who haven't studied Kwakiutl can understand something new about the way speech expresses notions of space and time. Maybe the author has gone further and posited something that shifts, if only by a few degrees, how we understand language acquisition. In that readjustment could lie a revolution in a discipline's thought. In order to accomplish this, though, an author would have to think in terms of more than the usual two dimensions of academic writing—page length and density of footnotes. The dissertation is usually the longest work the young scholar has ever written, an exhausting trek across the scholarly tundra. At some level, it's natural for that young scholar to see the dissertation's length itself as in some way symbolic of her achievement. After all, every book any of us picks up has a heft in our hands. A book is a substantial thing. Each writer wants her or his book to be substantial, to have the weight capable of conveying the richness of the author's thoughts. But—and it's the biggest but a first-time academic author must grapple with—the length of a book manuscript must be the *result* of the thought working inside it, not the thought's precondition. Nobody should set out to write a 350-page dissertation, even if that turns out to be exactly what the writer produces. In the early nineteenth century a German scholar published a dissertation in biblical studies that changed thinking about the composition of Deuteronomy. It was some eighteen pages long. In our day a dissertation on Michelangelo by art historian James Elkins ran to six volumes (three for text, two for illustrations, and one for notes). The length of a dissertation, however, has nothing to do with reaching a broader academic readership; real books are different.

Getting length right is only part of revising the dissertation. Moving from dissertation manuscript to book manuscript involves finding within the thesis what can be of value to a broader readership. It also means finding what will interest you, the author. This process is neither magical nor mysterious. It involves taking that interesting material you wrote and shaping it, lopping off the boring bits required to demonstrate how well you know your subject, and assessing the utility of all those different scenarios in which you apply your particular insight. It also involves stretching your interesting material in ways you may not have originally foreseen. Remember how Silly Putty, that venerable semisolid entertainment, lifted a cartoon image from the newspaper so you could stretch the figure into new and unintended shapes? The stretching was the fun part. In rethinking your dissertation, imagine your subject in terms of its plasticity.

But what can make revising a dissertation an anxious task is that it can all seem *too* plastic. There might be just too many directions in which it can go. When you wrote your dissertation in the first place, you had to fix its dimensions squarely. You decided that it needed an introduction, a theoretical model, a methods chapter, and four, or maybe six, analyses. You had to contain and shape your subject, and give it some kind of closure or you'd never have found the courage to write the thesis at all. And you did all this within the framework determined by your institution and its faculty. But revising a dissertation for book publication involves something quite different. The constraints you imposed to make writing possible now need to be set aside. The dimensions of the revision are up for grabs. A productive revision will feel like a set of "what if?" questions. What if I were to ditch half of what I've written? What if I were to rethink my dissertation in terms of chapters four and five? What if the really interesting area of my subject is taking place outside the part I've chosen for my thesis? This is revision, and though it's the toughest part of writing, it can also be the most exhilarating. Revision makes writing better. Always.

Revising for publication, however, is like serving two masters. From the perspective of the scholarly community, a good dissertation is a genuine contribution to scholarship or it is nothing at all. The dissertation must show that the author is in command of the material, broadly and deeply, and that he or she has something new to say. It isn't enough, as one professor remarked to me, to break old ground, though that is what a lot of dissertations seem to do. From a publisher's perspective, the good dissertation is a work of intellectual substance that makes a contribution to the author's field *and* that can reach enough readers to support the investment necessary for publication. There are all sorts of publishers for all sorts of scholarly work. But for the most part, they just want the best, most salable books they can find. Best and salable, salable and best.

To do this, publishers have to be tough-minded optimists. Editors turn down most of what they see. They have to. The number of manuscripts on offer every year is vastly greater than the list even the largest scholarly houses could accept. Cambridge, Oxford, Macmillan, and Routledge all publish well over a thousand titles a year, and even lists that large aren't big enough to take on everything that comes with a sterling recommendation. The ratio of dissertations produced to dissertations published isn't just about the editor's workload. Scholarly publishers survive, if sometimes just barely, by choosing good books they believe will work financially. Even the university press is obliged to make its numbers work. Though the university's goals and the goals of the publishing community overlap, only one of the two is a business in the most traditional sense. There are not-for-profit and for-profit scholarly publishers, but there are no for-loss scholarly publishers.

One of the things editors are good at is prodding authors to understand that a book happens only when a ream of paper, crammed as it may be with facts and theories, can reach a wide enough audience. The nice thing about a doctoral dissertation—and there is at least one—is that it is, in effect, a full-dress rehearsal of a book-length manuscript. By the time your dissertation is completed, it's been studied by specialists. There is no other time in a scholar's life when a panel of authorities will descend upon a manuscript, coaching you along. For the next book-length project he writes, the scholar will have to request that advice from an expert panel of his own devising. A dissertation committee isn't primarily concerned with whether the manuscript in question is capable of reaching a broad audience, nor should they be. That larger audience is, however, the sine qua non of traditional, print-based scholarly publishing. If you want to hold in your hands a book with your name on it, you have to think beyond the dissertation committee's concerns to those of the publisher you hope to interest in your work.

Academic publishers believe that scholars can reach more readers—even if that only means more scholarly readers—without jeopardizing the quality of the scholarship. "More" may mean five thousand more or five hundred more, but even the lower number may be the significant differential that separates the unpublishable work from the economically viable one. Revising your dissertation isn't "getting to yes," it's "getting to more"—more clarity in the writing, more clearly defined purpose in the structure, more potential readers. It takes determination to do that, though, as well as understanding that writing isn't merely the vehicle of one's information. Shape, voice, narrative line, density, length: you'll need to get these right in order to turn a manuscript into a book. Even scholarly work is subordinate to that great law: how you write matters as much as what you have to say.

Revision, then, is about second thoughts. Not vacillating resolve, but focus and commitment to all the things that go into the architecture of prose. You begin revising a dissertation by thinking about Big Questions. Who will want to read this? Is it too long? Do I have enough examples, or too many? Is the research up-to-date, and does it also demonstrate that I know the long intellectual history of my subject? But revision then continues with small questions about what goes on in individual sentences and paragraphs.

Revision becomes rethinking, which becomes rewriting. The cycle repeats itself, and this time you see something on your page or screen you hadn't seen before. It's an eerie feeling, staring at your work for hours only to exclaim, like Eliot's Prufrock, that this wasn't what you meant at all. But when you're revising your writing, that discovery is exactly what you hope for. You don't want to bask in the warm, self-satisfied glow of appreciation for what you yourself have just produced. Just the opposite—you're looking instead for what doesn't make you comfortable. And when you find it, you rewrite. You set about making an adjustment, and that adjustment can force you to rethink something else. It's not quite the domino effect, but changes at one place in a piece of writing often necessitate changes elsewhere. If Dr. Plum did it with a wrench in the Conservatory in chapter 1 he can't have done it in the Library with a knife in chapter 20. Ideas, like actions, have consequences. When you're rethinking a ten-page paper, you can hold the entire stretch of writing in your head. It's a lot harder to do that when the paper is four hundred pages long. To revise a book-length manuscript you will need blocks of time and plenty of yellow sticky notes.

Rewriting sits at the heart of revision and is inseparable from it. Revising means working through the details of those pesky little sentences while also thinking about the big questions of chapter length and organization. Like a painter, you'll need to get close to your canvas and then step away for a long view, weaving back and forth mentally as you solve problems very small and very, very big.

A caveat: some dissertations simply cannot be revised into books. As a rule, scientists don't revise their dissertations for book publication. Mathematicians don't. In these fields, scholars publish articles and research reports, and their disciplines are keenly aware of what journals "count." The same holds true in the social sciences and the humanities, with scholars ranking journals and book publishers according to how they imagine these imprimaturs affecting their own professional advancement. One of your options as an author is to turn away from what you have written and move on to something new. (My own dissertation is now safely stored in a heavy binder on a high shelf somewhere, and there it will rest.) Each writer will take a different perspective on her or his own work, which is why this book has been written: to help you do something, though what that something is only you can decide. In other words, this book aims to help you to make a decision, find a direction, and go. If you want to revise the dissertation manuscript with an eye to book publication, fine. The chapters that follow will offer you special help.

Beware, however, the common shorthand according to which dissertations are either "revised" or "unrevised." Two comforting choices, like the old-fashioned way of ordering coffee black or with milk. But revision isn't just one thing. If it were, everyone would already be doing that magical one thing, and every dissertation would run free. A dissertation needs some sort of reconsideration and rewriting, two separate but connected activities. That two-part undertaking is what I mean here by revision. Without it, the average dissertation is an impressively researched slice of the scholarly universe that makes claims on the smallest imaginable population of readers. Revising your dissertation for publication is about expanding that population of readers so that it becomes broad enough for a publisher to take your manuscript and turn it into a book. The unrevised dissertation can, in rare instances, be published, and I will discuss that possibility among others. But revision is, in almost every case, the inevitable step following the dissertation defense. Revising a dissertation is the means by which your doctoral thesis gets up and walks.

As you mull over revising your dissertation you will need to think a lot about publishers and readers. There is, in fact, no other reason to bother with the work of revision, since unless you keep publishers and readers squarely in mind, you will be rearranging words to no particular purpose. Revision is a process with a goal. The goal is transformation, and if you pursue this as far as you can, it means—prepare yourself—transformation from the dissertation manuscript into the book manuscript. Note that I didn't say into the book, at least not yet, just the book manuscript. Before there can be a book you need to produce something that a publisher can consider, that external readers can judge and criticize, and that you can then revise further before it is edited and proofed and printed and bound. Then it's a book, and only then.

This, finally, is a small book with a big purpose: to explain the sometimes subtle, sometimes crude steps that turn a doctoral thesis into something recognizable as a book. It's not easy to describe the process, either. Full disclosure: *From Dissertation to Book* isn't a cookbook guaranteeing that *any* dissertation can be published if only one follows the author's step-by-step advice. I don't believe such a manual could be written. I do believe, though, that something good can come out of any good dissertation. As libraries and academics groan that they have neither the money nor space for all the books they would like to own, scholarly writers need to think more than ever about how books can be made to work, both for the reader and for the publisher who can reach that reader.

As I began this project I realized that at its most basic, revision is a writing lesson. Write, rethink, rewrite, see larger issues, reshape, write more, rethink more, rewrite further. Repeat as necessary. Revision is all of this. In order to talk about the rewriting that goes on within revision, I needed to identify writing problems that plague scholarly writers, particularly those at an early stage in their careers. *From Dissertation to Book* isn't designed to help you write your dissertation or even to select a topic for doctoral research. But it's as much a book about writing and rewriting as it is about revision, simply because these are inseparable concepts.

Think, then, of this as a book with a twofold goal: to help you find the best outlet for your doctoral work and—much more important—to help you become a better scholarly writer.

2

Getting Started, Again

A young scholar completes a Ph.D. thesis and is congratulated by the supervising committee. A first-rate work, it deserves the applause. "You must publish this, Pat, and soon," one committee member says, and goes on to suggest two or three publishing houses to which Pat might now write. Encouraged by the response, Pat sends off the manuscript, fresh from the defense. Then the author waits, but it's not a long wait. The manuscript comes back from the publisher. The pages, which appear not to have been disturbed, are accompanied by a note. It isn't even a personal note, just a form letter. "Dear Author," the letter reads, "Terribly sorry. We don't publish unrevised dissertations." The new Ph.D. is understandably frustrated. "If scholarly publishers don't want what I've just written, why was I advised to write this, and to write it this way? I'm encouraged to publish quickly. My committee praised my work. But publishers don't want it. What am I doing wrong?"

The answer is easy. Pat wrote a thesis, not a book.

A dissertation is written under the watchful eyes of a director and an advisory committee. Sometimes that structure may be a burden, or even an obstacle, for the writer. Having the wrong committee can make writing slower and more difficult than it need be. But whether one's doctoral advisors form a well-knit team or a dysfunctional family, they form a support group, one handed to the writer by the university.

Once you leave the institution where you were awarded your degree, that support structure can seem, in retrospect, a great asset no longer in reach. Your university's requirements, down to the language of your dissertation proposal and the number of chapters your committee insists you produce, constitute a set of rules—a grammar, if you like—within which you produce the dissertation. That framework is both a harness and a help, and it determines the shape of an argument, the nature of the prose, the pace of writing, even the place where the writing will be done.

Pat, the new Ph.D. whose unrevised dissertation has just been rejected by a publisher, isn't doing anything Pat hasn't been led to believe is right. But the operating instructions of scholarly publishing rarely form a part of graduate training, which means that young scholars are usually thinking about the academic book business for the first time when the dissertation is already complete. That's late.

In today's market, even a first-rate dissertation may fail to find a publisher, at least on the author's first try. Who then is at fault? An inexperienced writer? A cautious editor determined to minimize financial risk for the publishing house? A dissertation committee out of touch with scholarly publishing today? The tenure system, with its demand for book-length publication in the face of increasingly unattractive odds?

Open Secrets

To scholarly publishers it seems that for generations, dissertations have been built on a surprisingly simple formula. Choose a topic, preferably one sufficiently narrow that no one else has elected precisely the same territory for exploration. Read everything written on the topic. Demonstrate, with less or greater subtlety, that you've actually done this reading via hundreds of endnotes, footnotes, and superscripts. Disagree with some aspect of received opinion about your topic. Document everything. Offer analyses that support your position. Although that may be the recipe for a dissertation, it isn't the formula for a book.

This isn't to say that dissertations aren't valuable works of scholarship. Each year graduate students complete interesting, provocative, even groundbreaking dissertations. Their advisors are encouraging fresh subjects, as well as fresh approaches. Each year dissertations appear that will become books. (Become—not are already—books.) To judge by the manuscripts that scholars send to publishing houses, the majority of the theses for which the Ph.D. is awarded are still highly limited enterprises—confident treatments of narrow subjects, making claims to boldness but doing so by means of elaborate reference to the work of others. The average dissertation wears its confidence and its insecurity in equal measure.

That mixture of diffidence and bravura shows up in almost all doctoral work. When a dissertation crosses my desk, I usually want to grab it by its metaphorical lapels and give it a good shake. "You know something!" I would say if it could hear me. "Now tell it to us in language we can understand!" It isn't the dissertation I want to shake, of course, it's the dissertation's author. The "us" I want the author to speak to isn't just anyone, either, but the targeted readership that will benefit from a scholarly book. The recalcitrant garden-variety dissertation—lips sealed, secrets intact—will find a readership among two hundred library collections at best. Most won't make it even that far, but linger at the ready in electronic format waiting for some brave soul to call for a download or a photocopy.

It's hard to pick up a dissertation and hear its author's voice. Dissertations don't pipe up. Like the kid in the choir who's afraid she cannot carry a tune and doesn't want to be found out, the dissertation makes as small a sound as possible. Often that sound is heard by a committee of from three to five scholars, and no one else. Revising a dissertation is partly a matter of making the writer's text speak up.

But what is it about the dissertation that makes it so unlikely that it can be made to speak? One senior scholar, veteran of many dissertation committees, cheerfully told me that the doctoral thesis was, at heart, a paranoid genre. "You're writing it to protect yourself," the professor observed, and meaning, too, that you are therefore not writing in order to create as bold and imaginative a work as possible. The dissertation is always looking over its shoulder. If you're writing in literary studies, for example, your dissertation may be looking backward to be sure it's safe from Foucault, Freud, Butler, and Bhabha, not that any of these worthies are threatening either you or your thesis in any way. To disarm your deities, you cite, paraphrase, and incorporate the ideas of leading scholars now at work. You pour libations to the loudest of the influential dead. The more you do this, the more difficult it becomes to see where your own work ends and the ideas of the Masters begin, so thoroughly has your writing absorbed a way of expressing itself. Then there are the scholars who sit on your dissertation committee. They may not be famous, but for the moment they are the Kindly Ones—the Eumenides—and you will want them on your side. These are natural responses to authority, to one's teachers, to those who will pass judgment on your work. All this looking over the shoulder may be good for self-protection, but it gets between you and the book you would like to be writing.

The Not-Yet-a-Book

Many factors militate against a dissertation becoming a book. Yet some dissertations do, and many of these have the potential to become quite good books, a potential they often do not fulfill. The process by which a dissertation becomes a book has several intermediate stages, the most important of which is the transformation from one kind of unpublished manuscript into another, that is, from an unpublished Ph.D. thesis into an as-yet-unpublished book manuscript. Each is by the same author, each contains many of the same words and ideas, each is unpublished. The first is a stack of paper an editor simply won't consider for publication, and the second is one the editor will look at with professional interest. You need to pique that interest.

Revising is lonely work, especially for a scholar trying to make sense of a freshly completed dissertation. Maybe you've completed your degree by now. You may or may not have a job. In the evenings, and on weekends, you're working on the book based on your dissertation. This thing you're working on now has no advisor, no committee. Unless you're already under contract to a publisher, no one is demanding that chapters of your book emerge from your printer according to a strict schedule. You might, of course, arrange an informal committee to spur you on, but it will be a committee of your own making, probably friends and colleagues corralled into reading drafts and chapters. As they read your work, they will be weighing both their words and the strength of your friendship. Unlike a dissertation advisor, your best friend probably won't read a sloppily written stretch of prose, look you in the eye, and say, "This won't do." A good dissertation advisor will say exactly that, and then go on to suggest how you might fix it. Unfortunately, that same good dissertation advisor may not be on call six months after you've been awarded your doctorate and are sitting down, by yourself, to turn a humble thesis into something glorious and public.

In some ways it would be simpler not to revise your dissertation at all and just begin with a fresh subject. Discard the whole thing—the research, the structure, the prose. Some writers do just that; picking up the Ph.D., they lay down the dissertation and never look back. One can even argue that it isn't a total loss, since what the student learned from writing the dissertation doesn't evaporate, and the expertise garnered in writing it will now hold the author in good stead. But a new idea is stirring in the author's brain, and this time, he says to himself, he will do it his way. It's my guess that many writers of dissertations wish they had the luxury of doing something like this—a great new idea, the courage to turn away from the recently completed thesis, and the institutional freedom to spend the next year or two on something entirely new.

Before you begin, you may have to do something so tough it can be crippling: overcome your boredom—maybe even revulsion—at what lies in front of you. Every scholar knows what writer's block feels like, and dissertation writers are a target group for this disorder, especially in the twilight period of postdegree revisions. After having spent so much time working on a long and difficult project, some scholars simply cannot return to it. Suddenly, it's easier to do nothing or to send it out unrevised.

Resist that temptation. An unrevised dissertation is a manuscript no one wants to see, but that doesn't necessarily mean leaving yours in a desk drawer. As long as your work has potential, you owe it to yourself to find out what it can do. Rethink, decide, make your plans for revision and carry them through. Until you know what you have, you can't know what remains to be done. Revising the dissertation may be going back to square one, stripping the whole project down to its chassis, or it might be something much less drastic. At least the material is familiar. At the moment, however, the thing before you, the manuscript that only a couple of months ago was your dissertation, is now something transitional, the not-yet-a-book. Once you can face your dissertation as actually something in the middle of its journey, you can begin to see it as others might.

What an Idea Looks Like

Like all writers, scholars depend upon words used as precisely as possible. In contemporary academic English, "thesis" and "dissertation" are almost interchangeable, and in this book I'll use them that way merely to provide some variety. A thesis can, of course, be a master's thesis or an undergraduate thesis, but a dissertation is always written for a doctoral degree. The dictionary's succinct definition of a dissertation omits any mention of a proposition to be defended, and length seems to be the dissertation's principal characteristic. A thesis might be very brief indeed. Martin Luther came up with ninety-five of them, and crammed them all onto a document correctly sized for a church door. For modern-day academics, a dissertation is expected to contain a thesis, that is, this lengthy exposition of evidence and analysis is supposed to contain a core argument. It might be said that the thesis inhabits and animates the dissertation. Unfortunately, it sometimes seems, at least to publishers, that the thesis—the heart of the dissertation—has stopped ticking. Argument gone, all that is left is length.

As they are bandied about by scholars, journalists, and the academic reading public, the words "thesis," "hypothesis," "theory," and "idea" have become hopelessly entangled. In the Great Age of Theory, that heady period from the late sixties through the late nineties, many a modest idea came packaged as a Theory, with bona fide credentials leading back to Continental masters. The humanities yearned for the authority of abstraction. The social sciences were hardly immune—many of the most important theorists, such as Pierre Bourdieu and Anthony Giddens, came from the social science world. If theory aspired to a condition of intellectual purity, or inspired thousands of scholars to do so, it was a condition impossible to sustain for long. Theories of everything sprang up, with a concreteness that made it possible for a reader to connect a Big Abstract Franco-German Idea with educational practice in Illinois or the use of personal pronouns in Shakespeare's late plays.

As theory became the queen of disciplines, it seemed that every young scholar was under the double obligation not only to come up with a theory, but to do it in a way that was—truly, madly, deeply—theoretical. A good idea might be an embarrassment when what was wanted was a highly philosophical examination of the subject, enriched with the work of German and French thinkers. "As Foucault has said," "According to Hegel," "As Derrida has written," became the incipits of much academic writing, both at the professorial and graduate student levels. Theory meant many things to many people.

Even today, many dissertations fall into the trap of making claims too grand for the evidence mustered by the author. All too often, a small and perceptive idea is dressed up in clothes two sizes too large and trotted out as a theory. Publishers understand that a graduate student needs to demonstrate what he or she knows. But the book that a dissertation hopes to become won't work if it appears to be a cottage built somewhere on the rolling estate of another scholar's work. It would be healthy if dissertations could be entitled "My Footnotes to Jameson" or "Two Small Thoughts about Bretton Woods"—healthy, honest even, but unlikely to win the author a job.

A thesis is a work of scholarship and argumentation, and its primary function is to demonstrate that you are able to undertake professional-level work. It isn't necessarily professional-level work in itself, though sometimes it can come close to that. Much is made about the idea of the writer's "thesis"—the argument within the dissertation—as if each of the new Ph.D.'s created each year were expected to come up with a blinding insight. It was never so. Most dissertations have been written on the shoulders of giants. Many do even less, and just step on the giants' toes. A wise dissertation director once counseled a naïve graduate student that the dissertation would be the last piece of his student writing, not his first professional work. (It was good advice, and I've never regretted him giving it to me.) Every editor at a scholarly publishing house knows this, and most dissertation directors know it, too.

A dissertation demonstrates technical competence more often than an original theory or a genuine argument. This is, in fact, another of those open secrets of academic publishing: a book doesn't actually *need* an original theory. It's often more than enough to synthesize a range of ideas or perspectives, as long as one can do it in a way that creates a new perspective (your own) and provides the reader with further insights into an interesting problem. As academic publishers know, the first book manuscript will try to make claims it can't fulfill. Your book does need a controlling idea, though. A thesis isn't a hypothesis. Back in junior high, when the scientific method first came into view, most of us tested ideas on the order of "My hypothesis is that a dry leaf will burn faster than a green one." Or "Snails will eat pizza." We learned something about method, even when the green leaf failed to burn and the snails ignored the half onion, half extra-cheese. The first hypothesis was proven true, the second false. A doctoral thesis doesn't test an idea in the same way. You couldn't, for example, write a dissertation that tested the validity of the idea that terrestrial mollusks will consume fast food; there are better things for a biologist to be working on, and the result isn't likely to be something that would make a book. You could challenge someone else's thesis—for example, the art historian Millard Meiss's idea that the plague in fourteenth-century Italy changed the way painters represented God. But in challenging it, you had better come up with a conclusion that takes exception to Meiss. It won't do to "test" the thesis and conclude that Meiss was right. And you can't posit a dubious idea merely to test it and find it wrong. "Dickens was the least popular British novelist of the nineteenth century." This is false, and there isn't any point in "testing" it merely to prove that the idea is groundless. I've offered examples that are intentionally exaggerated, but a more uncomfortable scenario might concern the thesis that argues an intelligent point badly, draws false inferences from good data, or builds a structure on a few readings as if they could by themselves map your universe of possibilities.

Some dissertations wrestle with their origins. Can you outmaneuver your famous dissertation director? Challenge the dominant paradigm in your field? Attack the work of the chair of the most important department in your discipline? Any of these forays will create controversy, and controversy isn't necessarily bad. But it doesn't mean that a dissertation that gets you into hot water within your field is automatically one that will be publishable as a book. Sometimes a young scholar needs to stage certain arguments in order to break free of powerful influences, and sometimes that will be liberating for the writer. But the contentious dissertation isn't de facto more publishable than one that picks no academic quarrels.

A thesis is an argument, not a proposition to be tested. A doctoral thesis, however, is quite often not an argument at all, but only a very small part of a bigger argument taking place in one's discipline or in American society or in culture more broadly. There's a tension here between the imperative to be creative and the need to take a place in the larger conversation that is one's scholarly field. A good dissertation director will skillfully guide a graduate student to a dissertation project that will give her the opportunity to show her stuff and not fall off a cliff or get stuck in a corner.

A good academic idea is connected to what has gone before it, modest in acknowledging the work on which it depends, but fresh. It's not necessary for the idea to be startling or im-plausible on page 1, wrestling for the reader's consent and winning it by a fall on page 350. An idea for a book can be quiet, noisy, insidious, overheated, cool, revisionist, radical, counterintuitive, restorative, synthetic. Ideas are as different as the minds they inhabit. Some writers find it terribly hard to say what their idea is. "If you want to know what I have to say, read the manuscript!" a frustrated author declares. In a sense, that author is right—if you want to know what a writer has to say, read her thoroughly and with care. But that doesn't mean that it's impossible to summarize her work or to find in it something we are happy to call her '"idea." Your idea may be a massive corrective—think of the work on Stalin's Russia made possible by declassified documents—or a study that looks at St. Paul's well-studied writings in what Dickinson calls "a certain slant of light," finding nuances and making small connections because you were there, thinking, at a certain moment. I keep an Ansel Adams poster in my office. More than we admit, books are like photographs, possible only because the camera and the eye were fortunate to be somewhere at the very mo-ment when the clouds held their shape just long enough.

One More Time

"Revising" can mean a lot of things. Most of us encountered the idea of revision back in grade school. Now I watch my son struggle with the concept, trying to revise a one-page essay by "fleshing it out with detail" or "providing examples." His one-page essay may grow to two eventually, but it will take a lot of work. Fast-forward to college, when papers seem to come either in one feverish rush or are written and rewritten again under the eagle-eyed supervision of a demanding professor.

Remember that mystery of college life according to which the paper written at 3:00 A.M. turned out, at least sometimes, to be as good as the one that went through four drafts? The parallel frustration of one's professional career involves the lecture written the night before turning out far better than the talk you researched for months. It's wonderful to have had this experience at least once. But the devil-may-care approach isn't going to make you a better writer and thinker. Write, save, revise, save, revise. If your Byronic persona depends on your not letting anyone know how hard you work, keep it a secret. But in the silence of your locked room, be as tough on your writing as you can. Remember that the very idea of revision—that something flimsy can be bettered, or that the good can be made great—acts out one optimistic idea of human progress. Revision is a job for optimists.

Some kinds of revision require the greatest skill, the subtlest ear. A great editor can tweak a good piece of writing and turn it into something that alters your metabolic rate. What Pound did for Eliot, what Perkins did for Fitzgerald and others, may be much like what unnamed editors at the *New Yorker* or Knopf still accomplish regularly so that what we finally get reads like a million bucks (and sometimes wins the author a book contract that big). Don't worry—that's not the kind of revision this book has in mind. You already know enough to take your dissertation to the next level. Deciding what that level is will be the first job.

To get started, let's crack open the idea of revision itself. To revise a dissertation effectively you will need to think yourself *out of one genre and into another.* The task requires a rethinking so thorough that it might better be described not as revision at all but as *adaptation.* Works of literature adapted to the big screen may bend the text beyond recognition (think of the sanitized endings in film versions of Tennessee Williams's plays, or *The Wizard of Oz,* which Hollywood—but not L. Frank Baum—tells us was just a dream). Others follow the written narrative with an acolyte's devotion (think *Harry Potter and the Sorcerer's Stone*). It would be the rare dissertation that takes on a new life as a film script, but it's a useful point of comparison. A dissertation revised successfully into a book manuscript morphs into a new genre. As you transform your own dissertation manuscript into a book manuscript, tell yourself you're adapting. It sounds grand, but it can give you a boost.

There are many kinds of revising. The sort of revision required to turn a dissertation into a book manuscript is different from the effort of revising a dissertation chapter before giving it to your advisor. That kind of revision is fundamentally the same process you have followed throughout your school years. It isn't much different from what you did when you revised your freshman paper "Foreshadowing in Greek Drama." You rewrote the essay, with or without the benefit of comments from a teacher, in order to clarify the order and presentation of ideas on the page, and somehow, as you did this, you discovered what you were thinking. The result was clearer. Whether the writing grew clearer because the thought was given a polish or whether you came to a clearer understanding as the words revealed themselves on the page is a question for philosophers and cognitive scientists. Me, I suspect that the ideas only agree to step out of the shadows when you take the time to write them down. Writing isn't a record of your thinking, it *is* your thinking.

The process by which a good essay becomes a better essay, a dissertation chapter turns into a better dissertation chapter, or a good dissertation draft a very good dissertation draft, is essentially conservative. You strengthen what you've written but leave the form alone. You clarify a scholarly argument but retain the level of discourse in which you first articulated it. You tidy up the spelling and grammar. You expand and polish your footnotes, and bolster a cautiously proposed idea with an additional block quotation. As you work your way through, you devote special care to the opening paragraph, to the concluding paragraph, and to the first and last sentences of each paragraph in between.

Revise the college essay on Sophocles and you get a better college essay; revise a dissertation chapter on lactose intolerance among the Masai and you get a better dissertation chapter. But revising a dissertation in order to produce a book manuscript is different. Conservative revision asks the same questions again and more pointedly. Dissertation revision, however, asks different ones. Consider these:

Who am I writing for now that I'm not writing for my committee alone? A scholarly book, like every other kind of book a publisher takes on, has to be written with an audience clearly in mind. Not only do you have to know who that audience might be, you'll need to convince a publisher that there are enough of them. These aren't impossible demands. A scholarly book is, by definition, a book with a limited but very real readership. That readership may be professors and graduate students studying primary school administration, or historians working on the role of women in the cold war, or well-educated readers within the academy and without who buy everything published on the cult of Cybele. If your audience is strictly academic, you can get a reasonably good sense of how many professors are teaching the subject. Your discipline's professional organization may be able to give you information about how many professors are teaching a certain course. You can also research the catalogues of mailing-list companies that collect data on who teaches what. One such is MDR, which stands for Marketing Data Retrieval. That there are twelve hundred professors teaching an introduction to gender and astrology is not an unimportant fact to have at your disposal if you are revising a dissertation on the subject.

Is there really a book here? Whether there is a book in your dissertation isn't a question to which there can be a simple answer. In fact, there may be several answers. There may be a book staring you in the face. There may be a book emerging from the alluvial plain and awaiting further excavation. There may be no book at all, but excellent pieces you can publish. Carry those questions with you as you think about your own book and read this one.

What is necessary for a dissertation but undesirable in a book? A dissertation needs certain things, a book others. Some things are necessary to both. Revision is cutting away and building up, rethinking, and rewriting. The completed doctoral dissertation is a book-length work, but not necessarily a book-quality work. This is a sober truth, but it can be liberating, too. One of the most difficult tasks before the new Ph.D. is the job of deciding what's worth keeping. All of it? Two chapters? Parts of three? Just the first, in which you lay out your thesis and method? Looking at the dissertation in the cold light of a postgraduate dawn is something like moving out of an apartment you're not sure you ever really liked. Do I need that hideous lamp? Aunt Thelma's couch? Take it all and simply refuse to decide? In order to revise a dissertation you can't *not* decide—that's what revising is.

New Wine in Old Bottles

Some faculty advisors have been rethinking the dissertation from the ground up. Publishers began noticing the trend a few years back. Maybe your dissertation director was one of the pioneers. At your first meeting, he closed the door and fixed you with a conspiratorial eye. "You're not going to write a dissertation, Jim," he whispered. "You're going to write a *book*!" The professor smiled while Jim caught his breath. Who, me? he thought. How could a dissertation be a book? Fast-forward to the present. Whatever may be happening behind those office doors, it seems to publishers that more and more professors are offering this beguiling advice. "Don't write a dissertation, write a book instead; get it published almost immediately; land a job and launch into Book Two—the one on which any serious tenure prospect will depend."

There is no consensus that this is how a dissertation should be conceived and written. A more traditional view of the thesis is that it exists to establish an emerging scholar's credibility, not to produce a manuscript with commercial potential. Some scholars warn that the two goals are inherently contradictory. Others sidestep the question of contradiction and view the dissertation as a series of scholarly articles linked by a common thread. For these advisors, the dissertation should be publishable, piece by piece by piece—but not necessarily as a book. Each viewpoint has its merits, and even the enthusiastic champion of writing the dissertation "as a book" might acknowledge that the noblest goals of scholarly research are not always the same as the object of a publisher's delight.

Some publishers will be interested to hear that a manuscript for which the author was awarded the Ph.D. was conceived of as a book from the beginning. If your project was developed under this new dispensation, and brewed to a secret recipe in an advanced department, it's a good idea to say so in a cover letter. Asserting that your manuscript was actually planned as a book doesn't guarantee that you achieved that, or that a publisher will automatically give your project more serious consideration than you might otherwise receive. But you may have written the unusual thesis, capable of reaching a market large enough for a publisher's investment.

Keep in mind that an editor sees scores of dissertations every season, most described by their authors in remarkably ingenuous language. Far too many scholarly manuscripts make their pitch by announcing that what will follow is something that scholars have not noticed, incredible as it seems to the author. What follows is usually hairsplitting ("Napoleon was very bad, but not very, very bad") or the investigation of minutiae ("the changing frequency of dependent clauses in Scott's *Waverly* novels"). Unless you've uncovered the text of a lost play by Sophocles or Khrushchev's love letters, avoid telling the reader that what you have has been, astonishingly, overlooked. Writers of dissertations are prone to excited and detailed descriptions of their work, crowding the first paragraph with Technicolor language. Academic editors are a savvy lot, and have seen more manuscripts than most would care to admit. Better by far to have an excellent command of mechanics, a sense of storytelling, and a clear understanding of your material. If you have these three, you can present your treasure to a reader without hyperbole. "A scholar," Auden wrote, "is not merely someone whose knowledge is extensive; the knowledge must be of value to others. One would not call a man who knew the Manhattan Telephone Directory by heart a scholar, because one cannot imagine circumstances in which he would acquire a pupil."

For any newly minted Ph.D., however, the dissertation is the key to the immediate future. It is, to be fair, also a burden. I've never met a new Ph.D. who spoke with enthusiasm of revising her dissertation—of her extraordinary luck in landing a job at the first interview, yes, but about sitting down and planning her revisions, no. The dissertation is the dragon that has to be slain. Thinking about dragon steaks is the furthest thing from the writer's mind.

Two years, three years, maybe five have passed since you began writing your dissertation. When I was an undergraduate at Columbia there were stories of legendary graduate students who were still toiling on their dissertations thirty years after completing their coursework. To my eyes, these Butler Library specters were indistinguishable from street people. It didn't occur to me that anyone might become so immersed in dissertation research that decades of life might drift by and the last card catalogue entry be not yet in sight. The only advantage these permanent library patrons have, one might feel, is that the burden of revising the dissertation would likely never fall on their shoulders. If you're reading this book, it's fallen on yours.

Knowing What You Have

Before anything can be done, however, you need to be able to face the text. Don't underestimate the difficulty of doing this, and don't think that anyone who knows anything about academic life will jeer at your reluctance. Everything you were merely, happily, in the *process* of writing is now *written*. It's not going to help to wax philosophical about this, but you'll need first to deal with the irrevocableness of writing. The unfinished dissertation is more than a draft of a very long document; it's an intermediate state of consciousness between your student past and the longed-for uncertainty of your professional life.

If dissertations come in a variety of styles, it's not because the writer has sat down among a list of options and chosen the one she likes best. Most dissertations are put together chapter by chapter, the argumentation and effectiveness of the small unit (the paragraph, the chapter) taking precedence over the structure of the whole. I suspect that many dissertation directors would be delighted to approve a thesis consisting of five barely connectable chapters, each of which is, however, easily publishable as a scholarly article.

However your dissertation came into being, you now need to figure out what you have in hand and how best to make use of it. Revising a dissertation doesn't automatically mean taking a 400-page thesis and turning it into a 300-page book. The first task before you is to figure out just what you've got.

Things that might have happened while you were writing your dissertation:

- You wrote two outstanding articles, padded them out into unnecessarily fat chapters, and buried them among three respectable but not very original synthetic overviews.
- You began with an arresting proposition, boldly laid out in an introductory chapter. The chapters that followed touched on the arresting proposition, but never really nailed it. You concluded on a prospect of further research.
- Against the odds, you wrote a book.

It's likely that you already know which of these descriptions best fits your own dissertation. Many a graduate student will have decided early that there are two strong chapters he might spin off as articles in good journals, but that the rest isn't worth the heavy lifting required to take it to the next stage. That's important self-knowledge. *The first step in revising a dissertation is knowing what isn't worth revising.* Some dissertations, in other words, are better left as they are or cut into pieces.

Some have the seed of another, vastly more interesting book hidden away in chapter 3. Some have nothing to recommend them at all and are best left alone while the writer turns to what he has always really wanted to work on instead. Before you devote months to revising a dissertation, ask yourself these questions:

Can I see clearly the possibility of a book in this manuscript? If you can see it, continue. If you can't, pull out the best piece of it and send it to the best journal you know. If it's rejected, send it to the next best journal *and do it the next day.* Continue down your list until you hit pay dirt. Don't waste the piece you like most. Give it a public airing, even if it takes you a year of rejection letters and postage stamps.

Will I need to replace half of the current manuscript with new material? If you have the time and the enthusiasm to undertake all that work, do. But is the "new half" you would need to write properly part of a new book project or best suited to this one?

Will an article or two look as good on my resume as the likely result of this revision? If you think the articles will be better than the resulting book, consider publishing the articles and moving on to the next book project instead of revising this one.

If I don't revise my dissertation, have I failed in some way? Not unless it was a brilliant, publishable work. No one ever complained that there were too few dissertations published. If your attention has turned to a new project, work on that instead.

A revision is a second look. It's not a second vision, no return to a moment of inspired rapture. A revision is about casting a critical eye at your writing in the cold light of a morning on which you have a job application to get out, two classes to teach, and a committee meeting to attend. All this to do, and meanwhile you still need to rethink thirty pages on Los Angeles public policy or the history of headgear in the Middle Ages.

Revision is unromantic, time-consuming, tiring. It is also the only way to make one's writing better.

Revision is the art of rethinking what you have to say again and again, and achieving greater clarity each time you say it. Every graduate student knows that the dissertation is written chapter by chapter, and that each chapter might require several revisions before a thesis director will approve it. At last the time comes when a full draft manuscript exists. Now the writer can undertake final revisions, and does so secure in the knowledge that the project is at last ready for submission in partial fulfillment of the doctoral degree. But any scholar knows down deep that that final revision wasn't final at all. The final revision is the next one, the rewrite that turns the approved dissertation into something else. If you enjoy revising your work, or can learn to enjoy revising, you will have discovered one of the tricks that can animate your professional life. Scholars train to develop complicated theories or to examine extensive or resistant archives. Revision isn't as difficult as either of these skills. Learn how to revise and you will produce a better first book. Remember it and you will enjoy writing the books to follow.

3

Nagging Doubts

There are a lot of reasons to go to graduate school, and there are just as many that motivate scholars to commit years to a doctoral thesis. One of the things academics are good at is coming up with arguments to defend a position or action. Unfortunately, that creative potential extends to coming up with arguments why one shouldn't put the time into doing something with the finished dissertation. Much too often, the young scholar puts the freshly anointed Ph.D. thesis into the mail with a generic cover letter, hoping that this message in a bottle will find its way to shore and the rescue party will be sent out. You can do that, of course, but your odds of success are about as good as that of the bottle making its way from the Caribbean to Palo Alto. The scholar who realizes that the odds are famously poor can easily talk herself into not doing anything at all. If you haven't thought of these excuses yet, you will. It's better to address them now. None of them will help you get done what you need to do.

The Best Reasons Not To

The manuscript isn't ready. No, it isn't ready, but probably not for the reasons you think. The new Ph.D. knows that the manuscript she has just completed doesn't yet sound and look like a book. But what she fears is that she can't go public with her narrow findings and dutiful rehearsal of established scholars' views. Some dissertations are not meant for publication as books. That doesn't make them bad dissertations, either. If you've written a dissertation that is, as the British say about the curate's egg, good in parts (meaning awful except where it isn't), be tough on yourself, pull the good parts out of it (tougher with an egg) and get them into print. Then turn to the next project before your word processor cools down.

If the manuscript isn't ready—truly isn't ready—you'll need to take stock of its weaknesses and decide how much time you want to devote to correcting them. If, for example, your thesis is an ethnography of state fairs, you might feel that the number of case studies on which you based your research isn't sufficient to make a book. Will you spend three more years touring the United States testing piccalilli and apple cobbler? Only you can decide whether you have three years to spare, and the funds to support your work. If a wider research base will make your conclusions richer, you have at least one good argument for undertaking that further research. Make that decision carefully. The same time can be used in many different ways.

Take a tough look at a revision schedule. Decide if it's doable. But it shouldn't take more than six months of hard work—a year and a summer if you've got a job. Some people have spent twenty years revising their dissertations, and one trusts that the results will be great contributions to scholarship. But I don't know any graduate students who look forward to becoming mythic figures of this kind. Get it done, get it done reasonably soon, and send it out to be considered for publication by publishers. If you can't make that happen, move on. Remember that you didn't decide to become a professional scholar because you had only one narrow subject to mine endlessly.

At the end of a long career, after many book-length publications, you may look back at the adventure of publishing your first book, the one revised from your dissertation. With the benefit of hindsight, you might wonder what all the fuss was about. It turned out to be a pretty good first book, and became the basis for your professional life and many of the books to follow. It was, however, neither the meaning of your existence or the physical embodiment of your worth as an intellectual. Don't forget that you are much more than it.

But if you're convinced that your dissertation isn't ready to go out to a publisher, and if that's your goal, get it ready now.

I can't find the time to revise it. The most sought-after new Ph.D.'s land jobs. No matter how knowledgeable you may be about your specialty, and even about broad tracts of your discipline, it's unlikely you will walk into a four-course teaching load your first semester and feel comfortable with what is expected of you. Course preparation, teaching, committee work, and the huge psychological effort in acclimating yourself to a new professional environment will all line up to rob you of the time you need to revise. You can't let that happen. The newly appointed faculty member is expected to be writing and publishing. If you had problems in graduate school organizing your time, you'll need to develop a system that will give you the hours you need each week to get the revisions done. Revision, like any kind of writing, won't happen on its own. Make time to get the revision finished.

If you're telling yourself you don't have time but mean you're anxious about the result or distrust your conclusions, that's a different though related problem. Decide what's keeping you from pushing forward, then go after that roadblock.

It's too long. If you think so, it probably is. Manuscript length is an overriding concern among scholarly publishers today. There's no right answer to the question "How long should my manuscript be?," but a manuscript of 500 pages had better have a good reason why it needs that much space. A double-spaced manuscript of 300–400 pages can be turned into a book that falls somewhere into the average length category, but beyond that safety zone an editor will be suspicious. In the case of a dissertation manuscript, one look at the final version, all 538 pages of it in a groaning cardboard box, may well be enough to send it back to the author, unread. If your dissertation opens with a sixty-page rehearsal of the literature on your subject since the Devonian era, you can probably drop the extraordinarily well-researched background check.

It's too short. This is rarely ever true, though sometimes a scholar will say this when he means "I got this past my committee but it still feels thin to me, and I'd like to spend another year beefing it up." The hardest thing to get from a dissertation committee is an informed, sharp-eyed assessment of how your project would stand up if it were published as a book. Easy for committee members to cheer you on—they're not going to do the revisions for you. Once your dissertation is transformed into a published book it will be judged against other similar books. No one will congratulate you on your courage in publishing a flimsily argued piece of advanced student work, nor should they.

Lengthening the project isn't always the answer, however. Many dissertations are structured according to a time-honored plan: an introductory essay that lays out one principal concern, and a series of analytical chapters in which the author explores her theory as it applies to specific texts, social environments, historical crises, or categories of knowledge. If you've written such a dissertation, the problem is not that it isn't long enough—adding two more chapters on additional texts or different historical crises is unlikely to make the difference here—but that it doesn't have enough horsepower. In a dissertation, horsepower is the bigness of the big idea, the strength and utility of your theory, or the sheer formidability of the raw data.

Adding another analysis to a collection of analyses won't substitute for a missing conclusion. Remember that most dissertations lack a conclusion. If you don't have a concluding chapter that pushes the book beyond its individual insights into a new arena, write one. Sometimes, but not always, the conclusion really is the payoff. For one sort of dissertation that payoff lies in demonstrating the implications of the research or outlining the applicability of the data or the theory to other situations. Sometimes the conclusion to a manuscript is only a coda to what has gone before. This tends to be true in the humanities as well as in what are sometimes called the "narrative social sciences": much of anthropology, qualitative excursions into sociology and politics, and that most humanistic of social sciences (or most social of the humanities), history. Such finales, which may be more graceful than substantive, are nevertheless rhetorically important. Books have shapes, as do arguments.

I don't like it anymore. It's that existential queasiness rearing its head again. Who hasn't felt a degree of exhaustion—even revulsion—at picking up one's recently completed dissertation? Not liking it any more can have advantages. It might be easier to look at the manuscript objectively now that passion has cooled. (There's no doubt that writing involves romance.) If this is how you feel, plan on getting the dissertation into competitive shape, then send it out to publishers to see if one of them can fall in love with your ex.

I'm on to the next subject and it's the one I really care about. That's great. But this needn't be an either/or situation. Having a new interest means that you're intellectually curious and energetic, though if you're telling yourself this because you can't face revising your manuscript, think again. Most young scholars will agree that if they could get their dissertations published, they would. The job market demands it, either for retention or promotion or the opportunity to move to an institution where the copier machines work and there are enough parking spaces. You can revise your dissertation and still be thinking about the next project. Perhaps you've had the experience of sending out an article to a journal. If it came back with a rejection note, you could have sent it out the same day to the next journal on your wish list. (That's what you should do, anyway.) If you're a writer, you write, and writing doesn't stop. When one project is nearing completion, you begin thinking about the next, or even the next two at a time. If four years into your first job you don't have a book under contract because you gave all your attention to the better book rather than the first book, you may find that the powers that hired you are getting a bit nervous on your behalf.

A book on my topic just came out from a major university press. The first time this occurs in a scholar's life, the effect can be paralyzing. There is only one thing to do in this situation. Get the new book and read it immediately, sizing up the author's take on your mutual subject, the differences between your projects, and what you might present as the weaknesses or lapses in the author's treatment. There are a surprising number of books published within a five-year period, and even in a single twelve-month period, that have common concerns and aim at the same readership. The hundreds of books on 9/11 or the Islamic world are but the most dramatic contemporary example, though books on Shakespeare or Lincoln or the 'Net or race in America are other subjects that seem inexhaustible.

Remember that there are always going to be many, many books on a broad subject. If two thousand professors are teaching courses on the American Civil War, you can be assured that a good number of them are writing books related to the Civil War. If your dissertation is in this area, you may find that someone has written something that comes close to your own specialty. But here is one of academic publishing's open secrets: sometimes a subject will work season after season because those who are interested in it will buy everything of quality that comes along. Some subjects command our attention, because of their historical importance or their contemporary utility or because they have canonical status within a field or the broader reading culture. As you set about to turn your thesis into a first book, you might see yourself as adding to the chorus, not stepping into the spotlight for the show-stopping solo. Of course, if you've got that big song in your heart, a publisher will love you, but academic publishers know full well that most of what they bring out, with the best and most optimistic of intentions, will be absorbed into the river of human thought. This, too, is publishing, and this, too, is writing.

I'll never be able to get the permissions I'll need to publish in book form. This is a real problem, and has stymied many an author who works on restricted material or other copyrighted work. If your dissertation is on the lesbian muse and your work extensively cites the poetry of Elizabeth Bishop, you won't be able to publish the resulting manuscript unless you clear permission from Farrar, Straus & Giroux, Bishop's publisher. It might not even be a matter of writing a check. Bishop didn't write a great deal of poetry, and if you plan to reproduce thirty poems in their entirety, FSG may simply say no to the request. Certain kinds of dissertations are exactly of this nature, which means that they may—and I stress may—not be publishable as books. But don't rush to this conclusion on your own. Before you shelve a dissertation that you think would need to clear impossible hurdles, check with the experts in the field. There may be ways to get what you need, or to reconceive your project so that it isn't heavily dependent on all those lovely passages.

I don't have the time. Yes, you do. Somewhere. You can find it, though, only if you have an idea of how much you're looking for. Like buying a car, it helps to know the price before deciding whether you have enough in the bank.

And the Even Better Reasons To

I believe in what I wrote.

I can share something that has value to others.

I want a professional life in the academy. And that means publications. The book that emerges from your dissertation can be that important first step.

4

The Basic Options

Your dissertation is a turning point in your career as an academic writer, but the turning point is a crossroads at which many paths intersect. As an academic publisher, my instinct is to cheer an author on, offering encouragement to make the first book work. It is a source of great pride for both an editor and the author of a manuscript when something that began in regulation dissertation form becomes the confident, articulate book the editor suspected was always lurking within. Nothing in my training or professional work would lead me to discourage an author from revising her work further, and in a book on revising a doctoral dissertation it might seem ungenerous even to contemplate the possibility that the best thing of all might be to stop cold and work on something else. That option, however, is one that every new Ph.D. faces, and so it belongs here, at this busy intersection.

A young scholar faces several options, and it's worth thinking about each of them, even if you think you have already decided what you are planning to do in the months after your dissertation defense.

1. *Do not resuscitate.* Avoid all further mention of this project and proceed with something entirely different.
2. *Publish the one strong chapter from the dissertation.* Forget the rest. Proceed with an entirely new project.
3. *Publish two or three chapters as articles.* Consider them to be the core of a manuscript different from the dissertation but related to it.
4. *Send the dissertation out as is and let it take its chances finding a publisher.*

5. *Revise the dissertation lightly.* It's in excellent shape and was consciously written to resemble a book in structure and voice.

6. *Revise the dissertation thoroughly.* Use its basic concerns and materials, but now show them in a stronger light. Conduct additional research to buttress the hypothesis. Write a real concluding chapter once the auxiliary material is complete.

7. *Cleave the ample dissertation in two.* Develop one chunk into Book A. Incubate the remaining material. In the next two years, conduct further research so that Book B can emerge from it.

8. *Put the dissertation aside.* Move forward, not because you don't like it, but because you have always been committed to another project and this is the moment you want to work on that one. Maybe you will return to the dissertation some day, but there's no rush. You have plenty of ideas.

You might divide these options up like this: If you hate your dissertation, choose Option 1, otherwise you have Options 2–8. If your dissertation contains publishable articles, choose Options 2 or 3, but if it doesn't and you want to do something with it, you have Options 4–6. If your thesis is revisable as a book-length work, decide between Options 5 and 6, but Option 7 offers a different approach. Note that not doing anything with your dissertation could be the result of hating it (somber Option 1) or of liking it but being determined not to give it any attention just now (energetic Option 8). The effect of laying out these options is something like a psychological profile assessment combined with one of those black answer balls that used to be popular at parties. ("Should I revise my dissertation?" "Could be." "Yes." "Don't count on it.") As an editor I often wish I had a reliable version of that answer ball on my desk.

Paths to Print

Let's take a look at those options now, one by one. First, there is the distinct possibility that you don't want to publish your dissertation in any form. This is a luxury in today's job market, as you probably know, and the decision not to publish any part of your dissertation is one you should reach only after having taken advice from mentors and professional colleagues. You might be nauseated by the sight of your thesis, but that isn't a reason to undervalue its contribution to scholarly exchange. Some writers of dissertations have finished up knowing they would not pursue an academic career and have instead shifted gears dramatically, moving, say, from the department of geography to cooking school. Of course, if you have lost all interest in the project, let it go. You might come back to it in a year or two and find in your thesis what once, years ago, inspired you to take it up.

Almost every dissertation manuscript has one terrific chapter. You can probably name your favorite piece of the thesis pie, and it's likely that that one is the best. Early on, you will decide whether to try to publish it or to hoard it up like treasure. There is no downside to publishing a great chapter in a leading journal. Be sure that the journal is an important one. Editors at scholarly presses are unimpressed by the fact that a writer has managed to get something accepted in a minor publication. Better by far to seek publication at the most important journal in your field. If it's rejected, the article should go out the next day to the second journal on your list. If you fail at the half-dozen most important journals in your discipline, though, hold on to the material. You might be able to make better use of it in the course of revising your book. Publishing a strong chapter in the *Journal of American History* or the *American Sociological Review* says something about your work. It also puts your name and your ideas into immediate circulation. As senior scholars read your essay they become potential relays to publishing houses, recommending your name as someone an editor might want to contact.

Becoming known to established scholars is, of course, one of the prerequisites of professional academic health, even the key to survival. When you publish, you broadcast not only your ideas but your name. When an article appears in an important journal, you get around. It becomes possible for an established scholar to know you without knowing you in person, and if the established scholar edits a series for an academic house, you might be invited to submit your dissertation manuscript for inclusion.

An editor can hardly complain that an author has published one chapter of her dissertation. But it does need to be said that many young scholars, having heard that publicity is always good, don't make a distinction between major journals and minor, or between one chapter and the whole five-course meal. "It will help spread the word and build interest in my forthcoming book," the author says. That's only partially true, and not true at all if the best parts of a narrow academic study have been printed in a major journal and subsequently reprinted in an edited book at another house. One should be chary with one's treasures.

Sometimes an author will find that two or three chapters, sometimes even four, can be carved out of the dissertation for publication as journal articles. Doing so puts the editor in the awkward situation of wondering who would buy the book now that almost everything except the index has seen the light of print. If you are able to place chapters in the flagship publications of your discipline it would be pointless to argue that you shouldn't. If your work is genuinely groundbreaking—and I mean if you are one in a thousand new Ph.D.'s—an editor will want to bring together your published essays, a gesture that more usually occurs later in a scholar's life. It isn't wise, however, to plan on this happening at an early stage.

Publishing your best chapter or chapters can create new opportunities for you. Invitations to lecture, responses written and verbal from other scholars, further reflection on the subject of these now very public essays can act as a springboard for a book the author didn't know he was writing. The published pieces become seed corn, and instead of returning the author to the home turf of the dissertation manuscript, now partially published, they impel her toward something new. It's not unheard of for an editor to contact a scholar on the basis of a recently published article. The editor may simply inquire what the author is working on, and then learn more about the dissertation the author is revising. But the editor may also suggest to the author a project related to the article but unforeseen by its author. All positive interest in one's work is flattering, of course, but there's something particularly exhilarating about being invited to consider writing a book one hadn't even thought of. It can be a happy, if unintended, consequence of getting one great article into print.

The option of the author sending out the dissertation "as is" presents an editor with a dilemma. It is an option, and one exercised by many Ph.D.'s, of whom a disproportionate number seem to be English speakers from outside North America. That fact may indicate that word is getting around the American academy: don't send your dissertation out before you do something to it. Most dissertations sent to a publisher without any revision whatsoever will be declined without further examination. Some few will be the subject of an editor's enthusiasm and the basis for an exchange that may lead to a book contract for the present work or, farther down the line, a contract for something the editor hopes may grow from the soil of the dissertation research. If you ask publishers whether they consider dissertations, they will likely reply that they don't, or that they don't consider dissertations that are still in an unrevised state. Implicit in the response is the feeling that someone who is asking this question may be very smart but unlikely to have in hand anything resembling a book manuscript. Better to say no, the publisher may think, than invite one more unlikely project.

Although there is little space in the publishing world for the unreconstructed dissertation, there are a few exceptions, and if you want to publish your dissertation without developing it further these may be your only options. Many presses have series, usually edited by senior scholars, which for the most part present the work of junior scholars. A dissertation can be publishable in such a series, though it is best to find out as much as possible about a series before contemplating your future with it. If you have good reason to believe that Professor

North, series editor of Studies in Absolutism for Southern University Press, will consider a dissertation, try contacting her directly at her university rather than sending off a letter of inquiry to Southern UP. In all probability, a letter sent to the press concerning the series will be forwarded to the series editor anyway, so you can save yourself some waiting time by approaching her directly. A related opportunity arises when, in some fields, a work is awarded a prize for best dissertation. This can win you a very attractive certificate and a book contract from a university press. If this good fortune should descend upon you, accept it graciously and agree to have your project published there. You will have other books to write, and the second is almost always easier to get into print than the first.

The other option for the unrevised dissertation is inclusion in one of the handful of publishing programs that actually invite dissertations. For many years Garland Publishing brought out series under the headings "Outstanding Dissertations in" such and such discipline, an arrangement under which a senior scholar would select the best dissertations in the field. The late Robert Nozick edited two such Garland series in philosophy. A few years back Garland became part of Routledge, and so I have been able to see how the dissertation program works. The advantages to the author include rapid publication and inclusion in a series edited by a senior scholar. But these are highly specialized works, not revised for a broader market, and provided with a no-frills trip through the publishing process. Instead of a print run of a thousand or three, such a dissertation is limited to a couple hundred copies in hardback for libraries only.

Light revision is an attractive option midway between wholesale rewriting and snipping out the choice filet for journal submission. Light revision is the equivalent of dusting instead of redecorating. Sometimes dusting is all you need to do, or have time for. But when it comes to rethinking your dissertation, be sure that you haven't chosen light revision simply because the necessary alternative would be more demanding.

Light revision tends to be most appropriate for scholars whose work was conceived from the beginning to conform to a book's architecture—an introduction, a substantial number of chapters thematically linked, an inner movement that drives the narrative forward, a satisfying conclusion or equivalent finale, a clear authorial voice, a subordination of footnotes and references. In other words, if you already have the structure and tone of a real book, light revision may be all you need to do. Tighten the controls on what you have already set in place, read through for remaining eruptions of unnecessary jargon and academic overwriting, and run off a fresh copy.

Beyond the light revision option is the realm of heavy lifting. Here the author separates the weak from the strong in the manuscript, and actively sets out to repair the damage, filling in the cracks in the structure. To do that, the author pulls the entire edifice apart, salvaging two strong chapters, ditching one very dull one, rethinking what further research is required to make a narrative line possible, and writes a conclusion where previously there had been nothing, not even a bright smile and a wave. Over the years I have heard many, many stories of scholars who spent five, ten, twenty years revising the dissertation manuscript. I can't imagine any scholar wanting to do this. Thorough, or deep, revision is an option that holds out the unwelcome prospect of researching the subject until body and spirit subside, but that's not what you want to be doing for the next decade or two. Watch the clock. Even as you are finishing your dissertation, other scholars are doing the same thing. Some of them are writing dissertations that come close to your patch in the quilt, and the longer you delay, the more material you will have to research. Besides, a dissertation, *like any book,* is as complete as the state of knowledge at the time of its publication. Your dissertation manuscript may whisper to you that its story can best be told with only a few years' more research, but choose to do this and you may find that you are running very fast in order to stand still.

Some dissertations, however brilliantly conceived, are historically bound to a cultural moment. The impending fall of the Berlin Wall in 1989. No one will blame you for having published *Berlin Against the Wall* before the wall came down. But no one will forgive you for publishing it a year after the event and not reconceiving your project in light of these momentous events. And so another, and paralyzing, factor (*I can't find the time to revise it*) comes into play. Not only do you have lots more research to do on Berlin, you up the ante for yourself psychologically, insisting that a book that has taken three years longer than planned must be that much better than the revision that could have satisfied you two years earlier. How much more extraordinary does an author demand a manuscript be when it has been in revision for over a decade, much less two? These are complex mind games, and ones best avoided if at all possible. Revise thoroughly, even radically, if that is the course you have chosen to follow. But give yourself a timetable and a time limit. *No dissertation is worth a lifetime of revision.*

The chapters to follow will discuss the work that revision involves. It's enough to point out here that there is a big difference between light revision and thorough, radical revision. Even the best dusting isn't redecorating.

Sometimes, though not all that often, an editor and an author confer on the future of a manuscript and decide that nothing can be done with the thing, not because it isn't swimming in ideas but because the ideas are pulling in two different directions. A long manuscript might, for example, nominally be a history of American tycoons and art collecting, but with three chapters out of ten on Henry Clay Frick. The author might be able to revise the manuscript into a book on Frick and his place in American collecting, though that might not have been the original intent of the thesis. Perhaps there is a book on the role of tycoons in American museum culture, and the beginning of a monograph on Frick. Neither of those two projects may yet exist within the dissertation as it stands, but once separated each may emerge in time. Consider all the perspectives that interest you.

A young scholar shouldn't take on two full-length book projects at the same time. Ambitious spirits will try to revise the dissertation on weekends and edit a collection of essays on weekday evenings. Having seen this heavy-duty commitment many times, I warn young scholars away from it. Editing a collection of scholarly essays falls outside the scope of *From Dissertation to Book*, but a caveat here is at least in order: editing a collection or anthology will take much more time than you expect, and it will leave you with less energy, as well as time, to make progress on your own single-author book. Whether you can afford to make that commitment so early in your career is something you need to think over carefully. You may feel that having that edited volume on your CV is well worth the investment of time. But it will get there only at a cost.

While a few young academics do take on two book projects at once, I would urge you not to follow their impressive example. Figure out instead which of the two projects is better for you—more useful professionally, easier to execute, more fulfilling—and put that one at the top of your agenda. That second book on Mr. Frick can wait a couple of years. Maybe it will turn into a biography.

There's a final option on the list: give the dissertation one last look and promise you'll be back. Sometimes there are more exciting projects in a young scholar's portfolio, and the work of revising the dissertation seems unappetizing by comparison. There isn't any reason why your dissertation must be the first book if you have something else you would rather write. But if your career goal is to become a professor, this isn't the time to set aside the completed dissertation in order to write that sonnet sequence or your memoir of growing up Lutheran in a Presbyterian town.

Don't put the dissertation down because you would rather be writing something else. Put it down only because you can write something on another academic subject that is even better than what's in your thesis. If you don't think that that's going to happen, and happen soon, take the thesis in hand and find something in it that can stir your imagination.

Every dissertation, however much we complain about them as editors, as readers, and even as their authors, has something in it that made the author think, "Yes, this is a fascinating problem to which I bet I can bring a new perspective." Before you decide to shelve the project, take a long look at it one more time. If you have decided, after some soul-searching, that life outside the academy is your future, you admittedly have little incentive to invest time and energy in revision. But if you hope to become a professor, you can't be cavalier about this lode of thought on which you've worked for several years. Even if the task sounds like cloning a mammoth from one eyelash, there is something in every dissertation that can restart its author's enthusiasm. Your job is to find it.

yourdissertation.edu

Electronic publishing is a vast and unwieldy subject, and far more than a postscript to this discussion. Dissertations, like other scholarly works, will increasingly be made available online, through arrangements for wide or limited access, and downloaded for on-demand printing a copy at a time. No aspect of the publishing industry is the subject of wider discussion. Protocols for documenting online material in one's scholarly work, incorporating the evanescent nature of electronic postings into one's research methods, assessing the authority of online journals—these and related subjects are ones on which it's difficult to say anything that won't be outdated in six months.

Basic research is, of course, essential in any field. One of the most exciting aspects of electronic opportunities is the at least theoretical possibility of making discoveries available more rapidly than ever before. A scientist may enjoy the luxury of working in a field where a high-quality journal will publish monthly, bringing his lab's discovery concerning RNA to a readership that not only wants but must have the information. The journal will be available online as well as in hard copy. In 2003 scholars began posting the transcripts of trials from the Old Bailey courthouse in London, giving not only other scholars but history buffs the chance to read what was actually said in court in the late seventeenth and eighteenth centuries. But on a much smaller scale, the same electronic tools could bring to a comparable range of readers the decoded text of a Mesopotamian clay tablet recovered from the looting of Baghdad. The technology does not discriminate between big topics and little.

But the costs of technology and its maintenance are another matter. It's far too easy to imagine that electronic publication is virtually cost-free and self-maintaining. Unfortunately, neither is true. Systems need to be managed, repaired, updated, integrated into other systems, and held by expert hands in a constant state of readiness for the next great electronic fine-tuning. As for the cost of electronic publication, money is saved in paper, printing, and binding, and in warehousing and distribution. Yet there are very real costs to a scholarly house, still responsible for selecting work, evaluating it, editing it and designing its format, creating an electronic file and providing it with the ability to converse with all necessary systems. Electronic books are still supplementary to hard copy books, so that the work of producing the book—the thing with pages—remains, even as the number of copies one makes of that thing declines. The electronic text—the thing with lights—isn't counted in the same way. It doesn't make any sense to say that you have made one electronic book or a million, because what you've created is a kind of Platonic ideal. What you can count is the number of licenses that you grant, either to individuals or institutions, that permit someone, or many, to access the electronic file, manipulate it, or print it. The thing with pages isn't going to disappear, because its versatility and pleasure are considerable, but the thing with lights will broaden our access to material and ideas that would otherwise never get outside the research libraries except on interlibrary loan.

Doctoral dissertations have long been entrusted to UMI, a firm that stored one's work and reproduced it for a fee upon (alas, the unusual) demand for a copy. In contemporary dress, the organization is UMI ProQuest, which offers dissertations electronically, along with the traditional hard copy alternatives of soft or hard binding, and the now practically antique options of microfilm and microfiche. Thirty years ago a graduate student would need to read microfilms or purchase copies of doctoral theses that sounded, according to the available abstract, uncomfortably close to his own dissertation's subject. A light-year away in pedagogical time, a graduate student can now log on and locate ProQuest's catalogue of dissertations, even enjoying twenty-four free pages. Best of all, in the academic version of Pay-per-View, the viewer can download a PDF file of the desired text for about thirty dollars. For a bit more, she can order printed copy, and for a lot more have it bound up.

In fact, for your dissertation the overriding issue isn't whether or not electronic dissemination is a marvelous new opportunity (it is). What's important for a young professional scholar is how the dissemination of one's doctoral work will be counted by the systems upon which he or she must depend. And in the first decade of the twenty-first century, it's still the hard copy book, the thing with pages, issued by a respected publisher, that remains the basis of hiring and promotion. There will be exceptions, but they are likely to be supplements to the hard copy publication (you publish in book form your groundbreaking study of Stella Dalyrimple, Britain's first female koto player, and then post online her transcriptions of Gilbert & Sullivan). Some years, or a few, from now, it might become common for assistant professors to be hired and more advanced scholars to be tenured solely on the basis of electronic files. But that day hasn't dawned yet.

Not long ago an author with a book in production called me to ask whether the schedule was going to hold. The book was due out in the middle of August. The author asked nervously if that date was firm. His committee would meet concerning his tenure review in the second week in September. Both the chair and the dean had to have finished copies of the printed book on their desks. It didn't matter that the book was already in page proof, which the author could easily walk across campus. Only the printed book counted.

As technological options widen and financial constraints narrow, more and more doctoral work will be granted, or consigned to, dissemination in electronic form. But scholarly authors and academic administrators continue to want books they can hold in their hands, books bearing the imprints of recognized publishing houses. If you are intent on an academic career, your first responsibility is to secure a contract for hard copy publication of your work. That might mean hard copy of the entire manuscript. It might also, however, mean hard copy of everything except the eight appendixes in which you record your statistical surveys. That mixed mode of publication—the "book" in print and the ancillaries in the cybersphere—may well become a more frequent occurrence in coming years.

Dissertations that become electronic-only text might be excellent but narrow works of scholarship, or worthwhile and potentially broader contributions that their authors declined to revise further. The hard work of revision can give a dissertation a life in hard copy it might never otherwise enjoy. If it also becomes an electronic text—at the same time or years later—you will have the satisfaction of knowing that your online readers are enjoying your ripest thoughts instead of green fruit.

5

Reading with an Editor's Eyes

The dissertation is the ugly duckling of the publishing world. There are many things about dissertations that are common knowledge among editors, and so hardly need to be said out loud when editors gather together. Every editor knows the moment when he hears about a project from an advisor, or reads a reference to the topic in an essay, and suddenly the cartoon lightbulb goes on. Editor gets idea, or rather editor realizes that an author has an idea definitely worth pursuing. The editor follows up and discovers, with sinking heart, that the project is just a dissertation and actually a lot less interesting than a brief description of it.

An editor asked to characterize dissertations would complain about how many of them there are and go on to offer a list of their characteristic defects. Then, perhaps, in the interest of fairness, the editor would conclude by mentioning dissertations that she or he has published. The editor would hasten to say that these were exceptional dissertations, or that they had been so revised no one would know that they had begun as doctoral theses. With the wonderful hindsight that characterizes most evaluations of practically anything, the editor will point to the prizes a certain dissertation has won or the remarkable sales it achieved, including substantial numbers sold as course adoption copies. The editor will pause sagely, as if the prizes and the sales figures had been foreseen when the manuscript first made its appearance on the editor's desk. But not even the best editor can predict which books, especially first books, will win an important prize, and all editors predict successful sales more often than their books achieve them.

The point of Hans Christian Andersen's ugly duckling story is, of course, that it isn't a duckling at all, but a baby swan. If the dissertation is really that ugly duckling, something special lies in store for it. On the other hand, it might just be a duck.

Measure and Sift

It would be nice if there were handy measurements that could guarantee that an author had prepared the manuscript in conformity with some sort of publishing industry standard. There aren't. You won't be able to take your dissertation to its intended goal, though, without knowing about the traps that lie in wait for you. These traps have been sitting there, patiently, since the day you began graduate school, and some will dog you—and any writer—throughout your career. Different writers have different problems—I'm not addressing here issues that face the non-native speaker of English, for example. But from a publisher's perspective, weaknesses in a manuscript can be discussed in terms of four crucial elements: *audience, voice, structure,* and *length.* No manuscript works for book publication if the author doesn't understand clearly for whom the book is written (its audience) or if the author hasn't written it in a way both appropriate to the audience and appealing to the reader (voice). No manuscript works for publication if the author doesn't understand clearly why the book's pieces follow in a certain order, or if the author hasn't given the reader ample clues to understanding the logic of the whole (structure). No manuscript works for publication if its author doesn't know when to stop talking (length). There are other things to talk about, like block quotations or dangling participles, but they are trivial by comparison, or rather they can be viewed as part of these four big issues.

These four need to be key for the author simply because they are key for a publisher, too. The process of selection and publication is about choosing that project an editor thinks has a committed readership to begin with, is written and organized in a manner that will appeal to that audience, and is contained within a page limit that holds out the promise of fiscal viability.

Knowing a little about the editor's work patterns helps authors understand why these four issues are so important. A first-time author hasn't gone through scholarly publishing's hoops yet, and the author of a brand-new dissertation probably hasn't even had time to ask any basic questions about how it all works. Editors at publishing houses want new authors to know as much as possible about the process, because the more authors know, the more likely it will be that the right manuscripts will be submitted and the more likely that those manuscripts will be in the best possible shape for consideration.

What happens to a dissertation—revised or unrevised— once it has been submitted to a publisher says a lot about how the publishing industry decides what to accept. Editors live with many dissertations; you live with just one. (There are a few brave souls who have written two Ph.D. theses, but they are made of sterner stuff than most of us.) Editors are able to make rapid judgments about a dissertation and its ability to survive in the market. This judgment is made so quickly that the Ph.D. thesis is likely the first submission in the week's mail to be assessed and, in almost all cases, declined. It is a constant source of frustration to academic authors—and to other authors, too, though they aren't the focus of this book—that editors rarely provide a reason for not carrying a submission forward. Publishing houses are narrow-profit businesses, and editors have heavy workloads. More to the point, there isn't any gate that limits the number of submissions an editor might receive. A history editor at a major university press, for example, will be inundated with submissions, and even the availability of an editorial assistant or two lightens the editor's workload only a bit. When your manuscript comes hurtling back unread it's unlikely you will have anything but a form letter attached to it, perhaps announcing that the house doesn't publish dissertations but otherwise making the point that yours isn't one that has made the first cut. An author will feel, and quite understandably, that without an outside reading, or at the very least the inside reading an editor could provide, there is no way to know what is wrong with the project. If only it had been sent to Professor Smith, the world expert in Middle Kingdom hieroglyphs, the publisher would see that my theory of the conditional verb will revolutionize our understanding of Egyptian stelae.

The editor has made some quick choices, which are reduced to a series of hurdles, each of which a manuscript must clear. An editor

1. reads the cover letter;
2. decides whether to read some of the manuscript, or in certain cases, all of it;
3. decides whether the project, if published, could be economically viable and would suit the house's list;
4. decides whether to send the project out for scholarly reviews;
5. decides who would be an appropriate reviewer, and who would reliably turn in a report in a reasonable period of time;
6. determines, on the basis of the reports, whether the project is academically sound;
7. decides whether to go the last step and present the project for contract approval by the board or approvals committee.

In most cases, an editor doesn't get very far down the list. That's a lot of steps, and a book can't stretch its legs to skip any. It may sound as if your manuscript has only a small chance of making it all the way to a contract offer. But much the most important of these seven are the first two. Your editor decides whether to spend time on a manuscript, and on the result of that primal encounter the rest of your book's fate will depend, at least at this particular publishing house.

An editor's time is so limited that no allowance will ever be made for a poorly presented manuscript submission. There are simple rules to be followed, not only for dissertations but for all book manuscripts. Take your own through the checklists on pages 131–33 and see if it's in shape for an editor's eye.

Aside from the issues of its potential market and its scholarly contribution, there is another factor in your equation: the space race. A dissertation is always in some sort of competition for space on a publisher's list. So in fact are all the other manuscripts and proposals piled into the editor's in-box. A dissertation in anthropology may be competing with a collection of essays by a well-known sociologist, an introduction to hermeneutics, a trade book submitted by an agent, the paperback rights to a hardcover book from Simon & Schuster, a half dozen proposals all of which are second or third books by mid-career scholars, and so on. No house I know of has an annual minimum quota either for dissertations or for first books. If other book types offer greater promise of success, the unfortunate dissertation will be crowded into an even smaller spot on the editor's desk.

At certain houses, dissertations are simply not accepted, and the press's Web site may warn you away with language just that blunt. As you search for a suitable publisher for your project, do pay particular attention to any information a house may offer concerning dissertations. "We do not publish dissertations" seems clear enough, but you may be able to submit a substantially revised version once you've completed it. A manuscript's having begun as a dissertation isn't publishing's version of original sin, as much as it may sometimes feel that way.

An editor learns quickly that a dissertation, even a spruced-up revised dissertation, isn't likely to bring in very much revenue, and that a dissertation will probably take just as long to evaluate, edit, prepare for production, manufacture, and market as would any other, bigger book. Time gets used up whether the project is small or large. At many houses, editors have some sort of performance quota. The editor might be required to sign twenty or twenty-five or forty books per year, without regard to the sales revenue each, or all, will bring in. At another house, the editor may need to achieve a certain dollar amount annually, the total sum calculated by assigning a revenue projection to each project contracted. Under such a tracking system, an editor has a motivation to sign larger proj-

ects, since a smaller number of big books can bring her closer
to her goal. It's possible that more dissertations are signed up
at House A than at House B, but it isn't something you can
count on. (And no, you cannot ask an editor how her produc-
tivity is being measured.) It happens that some of the most
prestigious publishing houses do, in fact, pursue the best dissertations available. They probably don't do so in order to fill a
dissertation quota, but when a major first book in American
history is published at Oxford University Press it is because
American history is a popular field in which excellent dissertations are being written. That press's tradition of publishing
in history has built relationships with senior scholars who
might then recommend Oxford to their graduate students. But
it isn't only the few giants who are successful. Keep in mind
that there are plenty of other houses, such as the University of
North Carolina Press, that publish wonderful lists in American
history. No discipline is in any press's pocket. Dissertations
take up an editor's time, but if that time is well spent, the result is more than a good book, it's a good first book.

Discovering Talent

One of the main reasons for a publisher to take on a dissertation is, oddly enough, not the dissertation at all, but you. The
editor with a keen eye spots a dissertation that demonstrates
the author's uncommon intelligence, and perhaps a particular flair for something that is of increasing interest. A sour dis-
position might complain that such an interest confuses what
is fashionable with what makes solid scholarship. Substitute
for the word "fashionable" the phrase "of increasing interest
in the discipline" and you have a less fraught description of
work that is somehow aligned with the intellectual momen-
tum of the moment. Some graduate students are gifted not
only with superior intelligence and research skills, but with a
sense of what is going to be interesting to the field in a couple
of years. Tricia Rose's successful *Black Noise,* one of the first
books on hip-hop culture, was written as her doctoral disser-

tation. That book correctly foresaw the climate in which it would appear. Many a graduate student who has picked such a fortunate topic may not be able to say why she chose it or even that she thinks it will catch on. But for an editor, this is the prize to be picked out of a stack of submissions. A scholarly editor's job, after all, is to select material not only for its academic quality but for its potential to reach more than a small readership, perhaps even a big one. A great editor has good connections and a sharp eye, and something else, what might be called a nose for news. An editor may hear about a subject from many quarters—at academic conventions, on campus visits, from advisors, in conversation with other editors—before a single scholarly book on the subject makes its way into print. Then a dissertation comes across the editor's desk and gives every sign of being the first book on the subject. That dissertation is one the editor will invite in for serious consideration.

The editor hopes to have found a book that, when published a year or two hence, will appear just as the subject makes its way into the larger cultural conversation. It will take that long for the book to be revised, reviewed, edited, and manufactured. An editor is gambling that the book will not be scooped, and that this will be not only the best book on the subject but the first. As every editor knows, it is good to have the best book on a topic. It is also good to have the first. Sometimes a book that isn't all it might be will be published because, by being the first in the field, it will garner wide attention and set the terms for future debate. These are no small advantages.

In publishing this dissertation, the editor is hoping for something else as well. A first book is the chance for editor and author to build a working relationship. It isn't an exaggeration to say that when an editor takes on a first book, even "the dissertation book," she is hoping that the author will have something even better coming along in a year or so, and that the author will be submitting it to the same editor. Every editor who takes on a first book knows that inherent in any budding relationship is the risk that this will become a romance on the rocks, and that the author, having had a boost from

House X, will take her brilliant next book to House Y. The potential an author exhibits for further work, or better yet for further work of even greater interest to a wider scope of scholars, is an important reason why a publishing house might take on his dissertation in the first place. Authors will develop views of different publishers over the course of their publishing lives, and that may well mean changing publishers once or twice or more. Some writers produce books that are more suitable to one house's list than to another's, and an experienced editor will understand that things happen. Publishing your dissertation with an editor enthusiastic about your work is the best possible guarantee that it will be well cared for, and your editor will hope that you in turn will bring her your next project. But unless you agree to this, no one can bind you to it.

Audience and Market

Audience and market are often used interchangeably (I use them that way, too), but in discussing the "who will buy this?" question with a scholar, an editor often needs to distinguish the idea of audience so optimistically envisioned by the author from the real (and much smaller) market of specialist book buyers, warily eyeing the goods as they circle Web site or bookstore window.

Editors consider how a dissertation will compete with other books, including other dissertations being submitted, in regard to the elusive question of market size. Knowing how many professors teach the history of American television is an important precondition of deciding whether to take on a book that studies the idea of neighbors and neighborhoods in 1950s TV. Because editors and their colleagues in marketing need to know this kind of information, it's always in an author's best interest to provide it if possible.

Having heard about a promising dissertation in communication studies, the editor at Midwest University Press wonders what the manuscript might look like. The idea of neighbors in 1950s television might go in many directions. It could be a cultural history of ethnic identity in Eisenhower America, or an analysis of the nuclear family, or it might be a study of gender stereotypes like the comic spinster. The editor may be keen to have a book on fifties television neighbors, and on the basis of your letter of inquiry invite you to submit your dissertation manuscript. As it happens, however, your take on the subject is pretty specific: you're concerned only with early fifties television shows, especially those that have made the transition from radio versions to TV. You argue that the visualization of people the audience was only previously able to hear creates a new sense of American identity. After your long introductory essay, your review of the literature, and a brief history of postwar radio programs, you devote two extended chapters to the television show *The Goldbergs*. Your editor had hoped for more.

In fact, you may be able to provide more. There was that paper you wrote on Fred and Ethel Mertz and rental policies in postwar New York. With some coaxing, and enough time, you might be able to write the book your editor hoped you had already written. But there are many mays and mights here. The manuscript you first submitted wouldn't find a market large enough to sustain the costs of publication, and the editor turned it down.

An editor's perspective on the doctoral dissertation is that of a beleaguered prospector panning for gold. Too many dissertations, too little time. The author of each dissertation deserves respectful consideration, and all editors strive to provide that. But often, the only way that respect can be accorded is to reject swiftly and unread a stack of unsolicited dissertation manuscripts. Promptness is one form of courtesy, even if a rejection letter is still only that.

Exhibit A

A dissertation is like a plant under a bell jar, flourishing in its microclimate. Replant it in the garden and it may thrive. But it might also succumb, killed off by the elements or crowded out by more aggressive and established flora. Wilde's bon mot about ignorance, that it is like a beautiful exotic flower—"touch it and the bloom is gone"—comes to mind. Many dissertations are perfect examples of specialized scholarship, but put them out into the wild kingdom and they will shrivel and expire.

The best way to understand the weaknesses of a dissertation is to look at one carefully. The one you look at carefully, however, should be one you didn't write yourself. It's pretty hard to be objective about your own work. Though it's a skill we all have to learn, when you're working on dissertation revision it can be difficult to stand back far enough to see the weaknesses in what you've just spent so much time creating. You might look over a dissertation or two in your field, not one that was turned into a book and published by Cambridge or Johns Hopkins, but an ordinary dissertation dutifully bound and filed.

Before you read a page, pick the dissertation up and hold it for a moment. If this were a cantaloupe instead of a cardboard binder holding tens of thousands of words, you could judge something about it from its weight. An editor will weigh a manuscript, too, in his mind and sometimes in his hand. The average dissertation will arrive at a publisher's desk with ample ready-made reasons for an editor to decline it. Being too long is simply the first and most obvious flaw it might possess, and the one that will most likely permit the editor to turn it down right away. If your dissertation is five hundred pages long, don't send it to a publisher, even in an effort to test the waters. Unless you have discovered an unknown archive whose contents will change our view of a period or major figure, a five-hundred-page dissertation is asking for trouble. Some scholars, aware that a visual assessment is the first of a project's hurdles, sneakily print the manuscript out single-space and on both sides of the page. This merely annoys an editor. Single-spaced text is hard on the eyes, and at least some editors find that double-sided copying makes reading disagreeable. British scholars often submit manuscripts to North American publishing houses on A4 paper, which is the extra long sheet Americans think was invented to confuse them. Standard $8\frac{1}{2} \times 11$ is better.

Next, look at your specimen dissertation's physical presentation, the ordering of information from page 1 on, the writing style, the shape of the argument. Take notes. If you're an amateur sleuth or medical drama fan, imagine that you're solving a crime or trying to diagnose the patient's problem. You're attentive, objective, compassionate, relentless. It's the way an editor likes to imagine she approaches her work over at the university press building near your campus.

You will notice that the dissertation, unlike a novel or a history, has a curious shape. The top sheet of a manuscript is its face, the greeting that it offers to a reader. Consider this example:

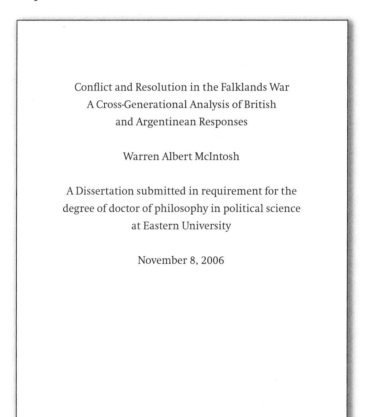

Conflict and Resolution in the Falklands War
A Cross-Generational Analysis of British
and Argentinean Responses

Warren Albert McIntosh

A Dissertation submitted in requirement for the
degree of doctor of philosophy in political science
at Eastern University

November 8, 2006

The next page contains the names of the examining committee and a photocopy of their signatures. To an editor this is a
sure sign that, even if the candidate is now ready for the job
market, this manuscript isn't ready for a publisher. As one editor puts it, the wounds are still too fresh.

In rethinking the first face the thesis will present, let go of
that top sheet. All an editor wants is the complete title and the
author's name. Put those two things on a single page. Don't
send an editor the committee's signatures. Editors are a trust-
ing lot, and if you submit a manuscript and claim that it is your
Ph.D. thesis, an editor will believe this is what she is reading.
If it turns out that you never actually took your degree and
are claiming you did, then, as Professor Higgins tells Eliza Doo-
little with a pitying tone, the angels will weep for you.

The shape of the doctoral thesis is one of its defining char-
acteristics, and one of its signal limitations, too. A dissertation
has a table of contents that identifies the chapters, but usually
tells the uninitiated reader not nearly enough about the
book's contents. The first section of a dissertation has tradi-
tionally been the Review of the Literature. As an editor, I en-
courage swift decapitation. Lop off the tedious summary. The
first chapter of Mr. McIntosh's dissertation begins by rehearsing ideas of intergenerational conflict during wartime since
the ancient Greeks. By the Enlightenment, he is up to footnote
194. By the time he reaches Vietnam, he is one hundred pages
into his review and his footnotes are into the serious three
figures. The art of scholarly writing—and it must be an art,
like any other kind of writing, or it is simply a dull rehearsal of
fact and theory—involves different assumptions at different
points in a scholar's career. Early on, the scholar wants more
than anything to demonstrate that he is in control of the history and breadth of his subject. The review of literature tries to
do just this, even if the result might resemble the Reduced
Shakespeare Company's presentation of all thirty-seven plays
in one short evening. Rehearsing the literature—summarizing
the critical opinion on your subject—can be thought of,

grandly, as an apotropaic gesture, which simply means something you do to ward off calamity, like making a scary face in the direction of a perceived threat.

The core of the dissertation is typically a set of analyses, one analysis per chapter. Elsewhere I've characterized this as the "thesis plus four applications" construction, and that is what Mr. McIntosh has done. After reviewing the literature, he proceeds to a chapter that lays out his thesis about responses to the Falklands conflict plotted according to (1) age, (2) previous military experience, (3) educational level achieved, and (4) gender. The following four chapters analyze the author's subjects, in Britain and Argentina, in terms of each of these four parameters. At the end there come the copious notes section and an extensive bibliography. As more than one editor has said, "It looks like a book—and yet it isn't." There is no overarching argument made available to a wider readership, there is no concluding chapter, there are too many tables. Mr. McIntosh's dissertation committee was very pleased with his work, but that only underscores the disjunction between dissertation and book.

By the way, no manuscript should ever be sent to a publisher unless it has been requested. Yet authors of dissertations, more so than other scholarly writers, persist in sending on their goods uninvited. In almost all cases, those manuscripts will be returned unread.

Listening for a Voice

Mastering an academic writing voice takes time and practice. It is possible to achieve a voice that is consistent from scholarly article to scholarly article, and from dissertation chapter to dissertation chapter, without ever managing to find the right style for a book. You might even find Mr. McIntosh's writing downright dull. Thinking about writing isn't enough. You need to hear your sentences, too. Read them aloud, and cut them to what is audibly—and not visually—a manageable length. Well-shaped sentences can be most easily formed into well-shaped paragraphs, and paragraphs with a clear order and shape lend your writing a rhythm the reader can follow. Too many graduate students aim for seriousness rather than clarity. Often, dissertations sound like prose under general anesthetic, working hard to separate the writer out from what he or she has written. This arid prose style is frequently confused with objectivity, and much scholarly writing suffers because of it. Objectivity is a goal of all analytical writing, of course. But even the most coolly objective analysis of economic trends can have a voice. Objectivity demands clarity, not obfuscation, and clarity is hard to achieve if the voice is muffled.

I warned earlier that revision is really a transformation out of one form of writing into another. That transformation might be thought of this way: *the dissertation is the historical record of others' ideas, supplemented by your own important insights; the book is the narrative of thinking on the subject, but primarily it's your thinking, even though it is supplemented by the historical record of others' ideas.* If this generalization is valid, it means that a young author can't write a book without risking intellectual self-exposure. That risk, by the way, is one of the most important parts of being a writer, even a scholarly writer. And it isn't the risk of being found wrong, for scholars are always moving an idea along by fits and starts. It's the risk of finding you have nothing to say. Learning to take that risk, even to want to take that risk, is part of a scholar's development.

Finding a voice for your ideas and a shape that will fit them, staging your ideas so that they develop a rhythm instead of moving jerkily like poorly projected silent film, this is what scholarly writing requires. Revising a dissertation, then, is about a lot of things besides getting your thesis into print and moving on to the next book-length project. Revision is a process by which your best student work grows into your first professional work. It's a way of learning how to revise not conservatively but thoroughly. It's an exercise that can attune you for the first time in your life to the needs of a readership and a market for your ideas, not merely to the articulation of those ideas. Revision is, finally, a way of thinking past the basic writing problems of doctoral work and toward a prose style that can make what you have to say reach those you want to hear it. If you can do that, an editor will not only listen up but applaud, too.

6

Planning and Doing

Revision gives you the chance to take a hard look at your work and face its weaknesses (and its strengths). Next is figuring out how to correct them and when to do the work, and then actually doing it. Highly intelligent people are adept at a lot of things, including making excuses for avoiding things they know they need to do. Even telling yourself that you need to do more reading is sometimes just an excuse not to do the hard writing. And what a perfect excuse! You'll need to be tough on yourself about this: the next stack of books you read has to be the stack you need to complete the revision. Otherwise these good friends are only enablers, keeping you from what you need to get done.

If this sounds like advice from a self-help manual, I plead guilty, at least for a moment, and ask that you hang on for a few more pages. Planning is doing, or at least the first part of it. Revising a dissertation manuscript so that it becomes a book manuscript should be a structured activity. It's too easy to think of it as the big jigsaw puzzle on the dining room table—every time you pass through you fiddle with a few pieces, and once in a while you finish a bit of sky or the edge of the house. But you rarely worry about deadlines with a jigsaw puzzle, and it's unlikely you will ever depend on one for your professional livelihood. Revising a dissertation is more like *building* the house, knowing where it should stop and the sky begin. Builders draw up plans and follow them. Academic writers are usually long on ideas and poor on planning. If you're going to succeed as a professional scholar, you need to become a planner, too.

Revision involves two kinds of structures: the present and future shape of the work, and the structured time in which work is to take place.

Time is an issue for any writer. There are some kinds of writing that have to be done in the moments between our other responsibilities. The novel or memoir you're writing on the side will have to be shoehorned into the time left over from more pressing obligations. But professional writers—and you're one now—are used to deadlines. Scholarly work is often written to deadline—the contribution to an edited volume, the essay for a journal's special issue, and the book review are all going to be fit into someone else's bigger schedule. It isn't a coincidence that certain scholars have their essays and reviews published with greater frequency than do others. It's not just a matter of critical acumen and stylish prose. One of the things that makes these writers attractive to a publisher is that they can meet delivery dates, revise quickly, and read proofs overnight if need be. Living with deadlines is one of those things that makes professionals professional.

Revising your dissertation is part of becoming that professional. It would be nice to have someone checking in on you every day, just to see that you got through the five pages you promised yourself you would redraft by dinnertime. But even if you live with someone else, it's unlikely you want to jeopardize the peace of your domestic unit by placing that responsibility on the other person's shoulders. The job is yours, and the timetable has to be yours, too—yours to sketch out, and yours to police. That experience of writing with the clock is key to developing good writing muscles. Even if you wrote your dissertation in a white fury, the revision of a book-length manuscript will benefit from having a schedule. Set one up. Tape it over your desk. Use it.

Here are some tips on how to plan out the time you need to ready your dissertation for submission to a publisher.

First, the schedule you build for yourself depends on the extent of the revisions you are planning. If you are writing for another sort of deadline—responding to a publisher who has expressed interest in your letter of inquiry, for example—you may already have decided on an accelerated schedule for the revision. Remember, though, that it is you who initiates contact with a publisher. If you're not ready to have your work reviewed for publication, don't contact a publishing house quite yet. Sometimes a publisher finds the new Ph.D. first and asks to see the dissertation. Enjoy the vote of confidence. Then take a moment to reflect on whether you are ready to have your work looked at by new sets of eyes. If you're not, reply promptly to the editor at Very Important University Press that you appreciate the interest and will be in touch as soon as your revisions are completed.

If you are already a confident and practiced writer, you may feel that you can review your own work and spot its defects. It's always best, however, to let others look over your work, even if you feel sure that what you have is ready for a publisher's review. The sharpest dissertation committee may not take you to task for style points or accessibility as firmly as they might. Remember that your committee know this field and have been reading your chapters in draft form. They are used to your style and have, through repeated exposure to drafts, come to understand your project's shape and assumptions. If they are the only people who have read your dissertation, ask someone else to read it. You needn't ask Aunt Betty—a fellow Ph.D. will do— but don't choose someone with whom you have been trading chapter drafts in the library or someone who was in your dissertation seminar. You want someone who can say "I didn't understand this," "I skipped the block quotations—is that OK?," or "You use the word 'liminal' an awful lot." Each of these responses tells you something you need to know, but they add up to one message: an educated person finds the material presented in a less than ideal manner.

A good reader can tip you off to words that clank, to paragraphs that seem never to end, to arguments that slice a fine point a mite thin, to the overuse of the passive voice or the semicolon or a favorite verbal tic. Your dissertation committee may have overlooked the tics and the rough patches of prose because they were checking that your data were properly handled (if you are in the social sciences) or was properly handled (if you are in the humanities, where you might not have data at all but theories). It is the next reader—the reader outside and after the dissertation committee's reading—who can alert you to writing weaknesses and organizational fumbles. Sometimes you need another's eyes to tell you that a chapter moves too slowly or that a particular discussion is distracting. Your response should be attentive gratitude. You want to know now—not in your book reviews or, implicitly, in a publisher's rejection letter—what your weak points are.

I like to divide dissertation revisions into two kinds: cosmetic and deep. Cosmetic revision sounds easy, or at least easier, and is. All dissertations require cosmetic revision. What manuscript couldn't benefit from a good blusher, after all? But by deep revision I mean a full-blown rewrite of a chapter, or each of your chapters. Deep revision of a single chapter might require further research to freshen stale examples or to help you find the conclusion lurking somewhere in your thoughts but not evident in what you have put on the page. Deep revision of a book-length work means rethinking your manuscript from first page to last.

I'll sketch out here one way to schedule the revision of a dissertation manuscript. It isn't the only way, and the allotments of time per activity may need to be adjusted for your project. Revision can take many forms, as can dissertations, which is why it isn't possible to provide a formula for all situations. Remember, the first thing to do after finishing your dissertation is to take a break from it. A month at least, and three to be fair to yourself. That break needn't be wasted time. It can be a good moment to have other people look at your writing and give you comments you will use when you begin your revisions.

Only some writers, and some revisions, will need to go deep. Every manuscript, though, will need the cosmetic revision. Here is a schedule that describes how one might allocate one's time in a deep revision (including cosmetic revision) of a dissertation manuscript.

Deep Revision

This will take time, but don't let it take more than a year. A re-vision, even a deep one, can be finished in less than twelve months.

Total time: four to twelve months.

- One month research time for each chapter that requires more homework prior to revision
- One month for each chapter that must be rewritten in light of that new research
- One month to revise an introduction and prepare a conclusion
- One to three months for cosmetic revision

Here's what I mean. The first thing you need to do is to reread your manuscript yourself, now in light of your own cooler reflections on the strengths and weaknesses of the argument, as well as the comments you have had from others you trust. Write these comments down. You might wind up with a short reading diary of your own and others' reactions to your dissertation. It might look like this:

Notes on dissertation revision
- Comments from Bob, Ann, Dan, Sally are incorporated here.
- Introduction needs overhaul. First pages too slow. Why such extensive reliance on Kennan in first ten pages? Idea comes through at end of introduction but the reason for the idea isn't apparent until the last chapter. Block quotations bored me, but I don't know if others feel the same way. Ask. Can I get away with putting the work of Snape and Finbar into the notes?
- I still feel that something is missing here. There is a story in the book, but I don't know how to get at it yet. Maybe I can move the middle of the intro to the end? I still have to write a conclusion and I don't have any ideas for one yet.
- The second chapter is the only one I still like. The first chapter should have been better, but I didn't have the time to look into more of the material I wanted to see in the University of Texas collection. Must find one week for research in Austin this au-

tumn. At my defense, Bob said this could turn into a book on its own, but I don't think I want to spend two years building a book out of this piece. Too many other things I want to get started on before the end of spring.

And so on. The objective is to get you to verbalize your response to what you have written. Some of the things that come out in the example above will affect most writers of dissertations in one way or another. How much and what to put into an introduction, whether there is a conclusion in the dissertation as it stands, which pieces you like, the relation of notes to text and, implicitly, of the writer to the established figures in the field, which pieces you recognize require further research, even where that research needs to be undertaken, and the matter of time. Everything in the writer's jottings needs to be thought through in order to revise intelligently and with purpose.

Thinking through how you feel about your dissertation is the necessary prologue to doing something about it. You may find it helpful to reduce your notes to a series of tasks. Such a list may look like this:

Revision plan

1. Clean up chapter 1. Watch tone, especially at beginning. No need to sound contentious when I can just respectfully disagree. Take time to clarify argument on pp. 13–15. Keep length of final version under 45 pages. Find a link to main idea in chapter 2 and introduce it in the last third of this ch.
2. Decide whether research in Texas will be possible. Can I rewrite this chapter without the archive? If I can and it will be good enough for a book chapter, why not just do that? This ch has always felt flimsy to me. If I decide against further research, this chapter needs something else. Develop a second line of argument or second emphasis. Perhaps bring in something from another chapter to expand what happens here.
3. Look at chapter 6. Should be two chapters. Not sure whether they belong here or should be relocated, but 6 is 80 pages now, and Bob and Dan say that's too long.

4. Is there any reason to keep 5? It always stuck out. Ch found its way into dissertation because Dan thought it was a great essay when I wrote it for his seminar. Publish it as an article and pull it out of the manuscript? Bound to improve flow of ideas.
5. Rethink what the book is about. Try writing a conclusion that pushes me a bit further than I would have dared. Build conc from material in each chapter. Avoid summarizing what has gone before!!! I tend to repeat myself enough as it is.

The amount of time you need to revise a dissertation depends on what you're going to get done, not on how much time you imagine you have until your semester begins. You don't want to do two months of revision because July and August is all the time you have, and then trust that good things will happen. A plan lets you know what you need to accomplish. If your time is tight, and you know it's going to be tight, a clear-eyed view will help you rethink the kind of revision you can undertake.

I've proposed above a schedule that gives you two months to research and rewrite a chapter where further reading is required. That would mean that if you have to re-research three chapters in order to make your dissertation a respectable book, you would plan on having rewritten the three chapters within six months, plus additional time for cosmetic revision and, perhaps, preparation of an introduction and conclusion. It's unlikely anyone needs to re-research every single chapter of a dissertation. But if a manuscript requires that much additional labor, there will be other major flaws in its design model. In such a case it might be best to think about focusing on one of those chapters, turning it into a publishable journal article, and moving on to the book you wanted to write while you were writing your dissertation instead.

Pediatric nurses cheerfully explain to new parents that, among other things, you need to keep the baby's two ends tidy. Your dissertation is a bit like that, too. Tops and tails, the beginning and the end of the manuscript, need special attention.

On the matter of introductions and conclusions, I allot four weeks. That's not much time to produce two pieces of work. They may look like two chapters, but they're not going to take as long, and if you think they are you may be misunderstanding what the introduction and conclusion are supposed to be. Your dissertation manuscript already contains an introduction of some sort. The goal of revision here is to make the introduction speak to a wider audience and to lure the reader. Even scholars want to be seduced by writing. The introduction needn't be massive, and it needn't give away the contents of the book itself. Under no circumstances should it outline what will happen in each of the chapters to follow. But the introduction has a job to do, and as you revise you need to keep that job squarely in mind.

Introductions: establish an intriguing problem or issue. Your introduction needs to demonstrate that you yourself are interested in what you have written. This isn't a matter of self-congratulation. Too often, academic writers hide behind obfuscating language and, what's worse, convey their own lack of faith in the value of what they have produced. Good scholarly writing says, "I trust you to read my work, and I trust myself to tell you about it." It's not self-inflating, not condescending. If you are a scholar who has spent a year, or four, producing a manuscript, you have something to say. In the introduction, you need to say that as clearly as you can.

Don't, however, give away the conclusion. ("As I will prove, Seneca's early diet has affected the course of Stoic thought for two thousand years.") You may prove this, and you may not, but a book isn't as elegant as a mathematical proof. The pleasure—yes, pleasure—in your writing is in part the journey you lay out for your readers. Your conclusion might not be watertight, and yet your analyses, your asides, your footnotes and bibliography could add up to quite an interesting book.

Your book begins the moment it opens its mouth. Which means that as soon as your reader has glanced at the title (so very important to the impression you are trying to create), flipped through the front matter, and landed on page 1, your words are in the spotlight. The introduction is as important as any analysis that follows. More important, in fact, because if you want to interest a publisher in what you have to say, you will have to make that introduction strong, clear, bright. Rewrite your introduction a dozen times if necessary, but polish it. Not only is it the first thing that an editor will read, it's also the model—your model—for the writing to follow.

Conclusions. Conclusions are just as important. Ginger Rogers said of her dancing partnership with Fred Astaire that she did everything he did, only backwards and in heels. I like to think of Fred as the book's introduction and Ginger as the conclusion. The conclusion has to partner the introduction and to mirror its concerns, its tone, the questions it has raised. A good conclusion might actually say "See, I set up a problem and I've demonstrated through six analyses that unemployment rises in inverse relation to the cost of bottled water," if such are the tone and the terms of the book that has preceded it.

More attractively written conclusions, though, *mirror without repeating* what has gone before. You want to recall to the reader's mind the voyage you promised in the opening pages. You are happy to gesture here toward some of the discussions that have taken place in the chapters that followed the introduction. But the conclusion then has to bring the book to a rhetorically satisfying end. When you listen to a piece of music you know why it ends when it does. Writing wants that sense of closure, too. You don't want to hide behind the dreaded words "As has been previously shown" or "As I have proven." The rhetoric of previously showing and having proven is a staple of dissertations, and for the purposes of earning one's Ph.D. many an argument must be shown more than once, and many a proof must be reannounced. For a publisher, however, these creaky structures signal that the writer hasn't yet thought about a readership outside the dissertation defense room. If you want to interest a publisher in taking your work on, you will need to present your concluding thoughts in a less ungainly manner.

In short, your conclusion is a place of summing up, setting

to rest, and ringing down the curtain. You may have a big finish, a chapter that reads as a grand finale. Here's where you pull out all the stops and throw out your boldest and most speculative thesis. But most conclusions, especially for a first book, are more cautious, and that's fine. Think here about the introduction. If you welcomed your reader at the beginning of your book, this is the point at which you are, like a good host, leaving the best possible impression as they depart. If your guests include children you may have some goodie bags on hand. A surprising insight might be the last gift you offer your reader before signing off.

This rapid description of deep revision only begins to map out the work that you will undertake. The scheme I suggest here may sound rushed, but remember that most dissertations don't require new research for every chapter. Once you have thought through what you must revise, assign a time to each phase of the work. Add the weeks up. You may spend eight weeks in deep revision or twenty. On the other hand, you may have spent none and decided that what you had was in pretty good shape. In either case, you now have the cosmetic work ahead of you.

Cosmetic Revision

This is the short course. Every dissertation needs it, and every dissertation can benefit from it. If you can't or won't take on deep revision, promise yourself that you will spend at least this time making your manuscript presentable for the outside world.

Total time: three months.

Cosmetic revision—here's the good news—is almost shockingly superficial. Writers are always delighted to discover that small things make big differences, especially when those small things are within their control. Think of how much difference a good new title makes to a dissertation manuscript. It might sound cavalier—even "unprofessional"—to admit one is doing only a cosmetic revision of one's dissertation. But I think there are a lot of dissertations being completed now that need just that.

In a month you can review your manuscript quickly. Dissertations have particular writing problems, borne from the simple fact that writing skills are not a high priority for scholars in training. It is easy for a young Ph.D. to believe that difficult writing is professional writing, and that academic work must be dense. While the dissertation is often thought of as the "quick" or "easy" first book, it isn't really either. Often the author spends too little time on writing basics. The manuscript is sent out to publishers without having been revised at all—not even in the most rudimentary, cosmetic way. Editors almost always turn these submissions down.

The simplest cosmetic revisions can be the most important. While nothing could seem easier than proofreading your manuscript perfectly or being sure that the finished version is printed clearly and double-spaced throughout, nothing will catch an editor's eye faster than your failure to have done these things. Do manuscripts get turned down because the author has failed to maintain subject-verb agreement? Perhaps not exactly, but hundreds of manuscripts are declined in a minute because they are sloppily prepared.

Every so often, a first-time author is shocked to learn that publishing professionals may not take the time to see past an awkward title, single-spaced text, and the occasional error in grammar. But why should they? There are thousands of scholarly manuscripts available every year, and editors don't have the luxury of giving special attention to the ones exhibiting antisocial behavior. Clean up your grammar. Untangle your overly complex sentences.

Cosmetic revision isn't difficult, but it's more than turning on your computer's spelling and grammar checks. In a month you can work through your manuscript and take notes on what needs to be fixed. In two more you can crawl through it again, now sentence by sentence, reshaping long paragraphs, breaking up gangly constructions, disciplining errant passives and other sleep-inducing constructions. And yes, three months is plenty of time to be certain that there are no spelling or grammatical errors.

The most cosmetic revision of all is the one that will make the first impression on an editor: the title of the manuscript. There are a lot of ways that a scholar can undo good work by lumbering it with an impossible title. Avoid titles that quote literature (and especially avoid titles that use quotation marks to set off the borrowed words). Shun titles that insert punctuation in the middle of words. (Re:Vision, De/Construction, and other once-new formulations are tired now.) Avoid the academic double-whammy of an abstract title and a concrete subtitle separated by a colon. "War and Peace: Struggles over Water Rights in Nevada, 1980–1997" is an unhelpful way of announcing what a book is about.

The dissertation title has its own peculiar rhetoric, with an almost comic tendency toward the specifically descriptive. There is nothing wrong with "In Loving Memory: A Comparison of the Growth and Development of Nineteenth-Century Cemeteries in Three Midwest Communities." An editor, though, will have another view. Which communities? Why these? What's the point of the book? The title, "In Loving Memory," is good in one sense because it is brief, and because it introduces the concepts of death and remembrance. But on the other hand what this book is about—the reason that the author wrote it and thinks that someone outside his dissertation committee should care that it exists—isn't clear until the reader gets to the subtitle. Then suddenly the book is revealed to be highly specialized. "A Comparison of," "Growth and Development," and the very precise "Three Midwest Communities" are phrases that mean serious academic business. Are there interesting ideas swimming around in there? There could be insights into how European immigrants conceptualized new relations to death and the past. There might be vivid stories and rich archival material. But an editor will see this only if he gets past the first page.

If your dissertation was very, very specific, and your revisions can only do so much to soften the harsh profile, you might look to your title and subtitle as a way of redirecting a reader's attention. You don't want to misrepresent your book, but if you can gesture toward a broader idea within the writing and research, don't let the opportunity slip by. Calling the book "In Loving Memory: Death, Burial, and the Ghost of Europe in Nineteenth-Century America" might stretch you—and it—too far. But if this title fits your work, you have at least found a book title to replace a dissertation title. An editor is more likely to pick up a manuscript with this title than with the one the author first wrote.

When dealing with publishers, titles count. Never let a manuscript get to the post office without a title that could appear on the cover of a book in a bookstore.

Revisions are about big things and little, master plans and niggling details. An author, especially a first-time author, will understandably be dismayed that an editor has apparently dismissed his big historical conception. The fact may be, however, that niggling little details got between the editor and that big historical conception. The timetable you set up for revision needs time for everything. Spelling and grammar. Sentences of a humane length and recognizable vocabulary. A writing voice that sounds as if it has something to say. Paragraphs that know when to stop. Chapters, too. Those pesky details aren't so minor after all. They deserve a place in every writer's revision timetable. Clear your desk and your head and get to work.

The next chapter outlines some of the bad writing habits that often mar good dissertations. Whether you're planning deep revision or a light cosmetic once-over, whether you are a confident writer with a robust prose style or a cautious, "disappearing" writer, you will probably encounter some of these weaknesses as you reread your work. Cleaning them up now only increases the likelihood that an editor will be able to summon up faith in your manuscript, and in you.

Getting into Shape

"Structure" is one of those concepts that seems to be on everyone's list of must-haves. ("The 2000s possess the most impressive length, structure, concentration and delineation that I have experienced in 23 years," writes wine authority Robert Parker on new Bordeaux vintages.) Like audience, voice, and length, structure is a concept that haunts the writer. It would be nice if each of these four ideas could easily be disentangled from the others. But knowing *who* you're writing for means knowing *how* to write for them, and that *how* includes giving your readers clues as to how it all hangs together.

Shaping your writing happens every time you put a sentence down; reshaping happens every time you alter that sentence. I won't know whether the reader will think my work has been reshaped enough to meet his or her needs, but I can tell you that it's been hashed and rehashed in my computer as I've tried to make the sentences work better and then the paragraphs and then the sections. I tend to work on the smallest unit first and build up, and probably because of that I wish I were a writer who worked on the biggest units, threw the grand idea onto the canvas, and only then cleaned up the untidy bits.

I don't actually think it makes any difference how you think about your revisions—whether you see yourself working inside out or outside in. The important thing is that you value the revision process as a means of producing something that is better (better because clearer) than the last time you strung words together to make an idea. Clear writing displays the organization of your thinking. Clear writing is the organization of your thinking. That's what structure means.

A big secret for revising dissertations is that you can cheat a bit and still make great strides. First impressions are important, particularly when you're jockeying for a few precious minutes of an editor's attention. As you revise, you will be striving to win the attention first of an editor, then of press advisors, and finally of that elusive, invisible individual who picks up your printed book. Your manuscript must, at first encounter, convey an *appearance* of readability. That is, an interesting manuscript that is handsomely written might never make the editor's first cut if the project gives the wrong signals. The manuscript's title and subtitle should be your first allies. Chapter lengths, chapter titles, and the arrangement of the table of contents should also be on your side. Superficial details, you may say, but if you do nothing else with your dissertation, revise these trivial elements and you will have greatly increased the chance that an editor will go on to read some of the text.

Structure can't be a secret. It isn't enough to plead that an attentive reader will understand what you were up to by the time she finishes the manuscript. Figuring out the project's architecture isn't the reader's job, it's yours. Err on the side of caution: make your structure as clear and as useful to the reader as you can so that your ideas can breathe and move.

Writing structure is about order, a sequence of developments, and the sticky glue holding the individual bits together. That sticky stuff is the coherence of your writing. It's more than logical argumentation, though it requires that. Because they are often conceived as semi-independent analyses or case studies, dissertations are often weak on coherence. When we think of a scholarly book as unreadable, it rarely means that we couldn't read it if we wanted to. We might mean that it is so obscurely written that reading it would be unrewarding. But we might just as well mean that it seems in some way incoherent in the literal sense of that word, the pieces not cohering to one another. Revising your dissertation is in part about creating a bigger picture from several smaller ones.

Dissertations often grow piecemeal, inside the heads of inexperienced writers. How one gets from page 1 to page 290 can be more a matter of accretion than planning, like a mollusk girding itself with calcifying layers. Sometimes a dissertation can be laid out in the author's mind with the remorseless drive of a new superhighway and yet still seem confusingly organized to a reader. What's clear to you may not be clear to anyone else.

Making semi-independent chapters cohere might require you to split them into smaller pieces. It will almost certainly require you to rethink the names of the parts. While the duty to ensure coherence and structure is especially relevant for anyone revising a dissertation, it really applies to any piece of writing. It certainly applies to fiction, where a reader will have come to a definite view of whether or not the book's plot "worked." Scholars rarely think about plot, unless of course they are in literature departments, where the plot of a novel might be something to be analyzed. But why not apply it to scholarly writing, too? One professor of literature told me that she sometimes asks a student what the "plot" of a seminar paper is. Packed into that question is a keen understanding of how even academic writing requires a narrative structure leading the reader to an endpoint where something has to happen.

Every successful work of nonfiction has some kind of shape and a propulsive drive. There is an internal shape—the way in which the author has staged and developed her arguments, something we describe, inadequately, as "logical." But a book has an external shape, too, a kind of carapace that gives us our first impression of the ideas within and the way the author has arranged for them to speak. That's the superficial part of shaping your book. It doesn't substitute for deep and careful argumentation, and it isn't meant to. But the two are twinned; revise to create the outward impression of order and movement and you're going to see what you need to do internally (at the level of the chapter, the paragraph, the sentence) to make good on those promises.

The Throughline

Revising a dissertation demands attention to a narrative drive I'll call here (with a nod to Stanislavski) throughline. The throughline pulls the reader through the text, from first page to last, and at the same time pulls the reader through the argument. All good writing has it. The throughline is that pulse of energy along which chapters, paragraphs, and even sentences are organized. Writers of thrillers know how to use throughline better than writers in any other genre. Even if you don't enjoy regular-Joe-vs.-international-menace popular fiction, you can't but admire the writer's ability to keep the story going. Sometimes the result is all propulsive drive and little art, but so what? The treatment is appropriate to the genre, and millions of readers turn the pages happily.

The throughline of a scholarly book has a rather lower temperature than this season's novel about vampires, asteroids, the CIA, and one brave young law clerk. For you, the throughline is the logical organization of your ideas into words and pages. If you write with a sense that what comes next has to come next or the reader won't understand what comes before, you are writing with attention to throughline.

Some books are arranged along a series of historical events. Historians are envied for the apparent logic of their subjects, though that envy misunderstands the complexity of historical writing. Yet any study that depends upon chronology (an anthropologist's take on three generations of sharecroppers in Poke Bonnet, West Virginia) enjoys the built-in advantage of a timeline. Though it's possible to write a truly uninteresting dissertation in history, as in any other field, at least in the first instance the young historian enjoys this architectural advantage. In the social or behavioral sciences, a dissertation may more often examine a series of events, conditions, or individuals existing all at one time (the lives of retired furriers in Ozone Park, New York; the arguments for and against the inclusion of certain clinical dysfunctions in DSM-IV).

In other disciplines, such as philosophy or the literatures, neither of these temporal structures may fit. A manuscript on the idea of queasiness in modern thought might begin with Sartre's *Nausea,* but could go in any number of directions, unencumbered by chronology. The point, of course, isn't that the history manuscript will necessarily be of more interest than the philosophy project, but only that different fields have different relationships to narrative. Graduate students learn how their fields create narrative and mimic the examples they see offered as professional models. As you revise, choose the best possible models.

Singing teachers have to invent metaphors to describe what a student should do. Other than palpating the throat or the stomach muscles, a voice coach has limited ways of conveying the technical requirements of producing a beautiful vocal line. "Listen," the voice teacher says. "Listen," the writing teacher says, too. Voice teachers have long used the image of pearls on a string to describe notes in a musical line, each pearl-like note as perfect and round and as lovely as the singer can manage, each quite independent yet connected to the note before it and the note that follows. It might be easier to make use of this image if you're practicing a Mozart aria than if you're revising your dissertation, but each part of a book manuscript should have a shape, and, so shaped, each should connect to what precedes and what follows. Chapters are your pearl-like notes. Paragraphs are, too. Listening to one's own writing out loud is the best way to hear what one's prose sounds like. Find a quiet space, read your prose, and stop whenever you can't follow what you've just read. Stop, too, if the sentence is so long you begin gasping for air.

Throughline is developed in a number of ways. Consider your title along with the subtitle, its optional sidekick. Reexamine the names of your chapters. See if you've encumbered your fresh insights with dusty rehearsals of your field's development. Pull the table of contents apart and rebuild it so that it shows off more clearly what's inside the manuscript. Walk through chapters and notice where you get tired. Post directions or rethink chapter 3 into two more enjoyable strolls.

Go back and rethink your table of contents once again. Finally, rewrite the introduction. It shouldn't be the same book any more.

Book Titles and Chapter Titles

Dissertation titles are the butt of many jokes, but they aren't funny to the author. Some dissertations give the impression they were named by clinicians in white coats, determined to provide as technical a description of the contents as language will permit. Others dissertation titles soar into abstraction as if the goal were to conceal the manuscript's subject, and maybe even the discipline in which it was written.

Many writers use the title as a place to be creative, and then a subtitle as the down-to-earth announcement of the manuscript's real intention. This two-fisted strategy is well known to editors. The two halves must feel connected, however. Nothing produces fits of giggles quite like the incongruous linking of title and subtitle in a doctoral thesis.

A revision of a dissertation needn't have the same title as the dissertation itself. In fact, it shouldn't. The dissertation and its subsequent revision are for different audiences, so title them differently. Steer away from quotations from literature, phrases well known from other contexts, and humor. (Even if your dissertation's title employed one of these devices, drop it now.) If you're not sure what a book title should sound like, spend an afternoon in a first-rate bookstore. Look at books like your own, or at least ones written at a comparable level of intellectual sophistication. Notice what works for you; try not to copy, but listen to rhythm and tone. If you get stuck, do what many editors do when trying to help an author come up with a title: look through what you've already written and put your own words to use. Be sure to read your title and subtitle out loud. Sometimes words on the page don't make sense in the mouth or ear.

Even seasoned academics can have trouble choosing titles.

Some years ago I was working with the literary critic Nina Auerbach. She was having difficulty coming up with a title for a book on Victorian women. The problem, of course, was that she knew her material too well. When I had read through the manuscript, a number of her own phrases jumped out at me. One, "romantic imprisonment," seemed right, and we decided to use it for the title of a book on "women and other glorified outcasts" (another phrase that became the subtitle). Like Poe's purloined letter, the object the author had been looking for was in plain view all the time.

Remember that no one outside your committee knows what your dissertation was called until you tell them. If you revise your dissertation and retitle it, no one will complain that it now sounds intriguing. An editor might pore over your CV and notice that your dissertation, written on a subject rather similar to your book manuscript, had had a distinctly uninteresting title. Don't flinch. Reply brightly that you've thoroughly reconceived the doctoral thesis, which is why it now has a different title. If in revising your dissertation you stumbled upon the first-rate book you didn't know you were writing, who can complain?

Think of the title of a chapter as an opportunity for a new beginning. Books, with their divisions into chapters, are already structured to give the reader just that sense of the new. Take advantage of it. Unfortunately, dissertation chapters often sound more like articles than integrated elements in a book-length narrative. A chapter entitled "The Heart of the Matter: The Thematics of Cardiac Arrest in Courtly Love Lyrics of the Languedoc" replicates the classic general/specific move of many dissertations. While you might look forward to seeing this title above your name in the special Medieval Issue of *Graham Greene Quarterly,* it may not be the best choice for the chapter of a book. Solve the question by looking to the larger context (the book), not the smaller (the chapter itself). You may be sacrificing your all-time favorite article title, but you may gain something more important. Besides, by the time you've finished restudying your dissertation, that chapter may not make any sense as originally conceived and may be rewritten into an entirely different shape.

Avoid titling consecutive chapters as if they were movie sequels, as in this example from *Gray: The Death of Color and the Birth of Modern Civilization:*

Chapter One	Those Gaudy Mesopotamians	11
Chapter Two	The Greeks (I)	51
Chapter Three	The Greeks (II)	96
Chapter Four	The Romans (I)	134
Chapter Five	The Romans (II)	177

And so on. While there are good books on my shelf that have used this layout to present their information, this is an uningratiating move for a young scholar. A reader would like to know just what is going to distinguish "The Greeks (I)" from "The Greeks (II)." An editor may suspect the author hasn't a clear structure in mind, and that's a signal you don't want to give. Better to create distinct chapter titles:

Chapter One	The Gaudy Life of Mesopotamian Civilizations	11
Chapter Two	The Polychromatic Ideal in Greek Art	51
Chapter Three	The Decline of Color and the Rise of Hellenistic Pastels	96
Chapter Four	The Roman Invention of Beige	134
Chapter Five	The Late Empire and the Triumph of Taupe	177

Getting titles right is only part of the larger job of finding, and announcing, your work's shape. Book title, subtitle, and chapter titles precipitate information to a reader. But a book needs more. Your dissertation committee doesn't need much direction to read your work, since they've been in on it from its inception. But a revised dissertation may turn into a book, and books need to be clearly mapped to be of use. In revising, you will seek to find the map within what you wrote.

If your dissertation has a diachronic form, your map has already been drafted for you. One event or period follows another, and along that axis you hang your argument. If your dissertation is synchronic, there may be some other obvious organizing principle—geography, say—that has taken you from chapter to chapter. Time and space are pretty big concepts, but like thematic or theoretical issues, you can regard them as strong threads that run through your thesis. No matter what the original structure of your dissertation, there have to be concerns that will keep a reader interested, and these concerns need to be emphasized in revision. In this sense, a dissertation is like a complex piece of music; your task in revising is to make the major themes sing out. Don't let the fiddly bits in the right hand mask the melody in the left. As you revise your dissertation (or in fact any book-length manuscript), think about the large organizing principles in your writing. Bring them out.

Accentuating the melody is one way of clarifying the themes of your work. As a result of having been built piecemeal, dissertations often have multiple themes and concerns with the result that what the author "really wanted to say" may have been lost somewhere along the road. As you revise, think—out loud if need be—about what brings these considerations and analyses together. A dissertation doesn't become a book until the author has a mental map of the project. Mapping a piece of writing means understanding the order of its argument and the presentation of its materials. It may sound obvious to say that the author needs to understand a manuscript's structure, but it's common for academic authors to assume that the complexity of the thinking is its own reward. The recent Ph.D. should take heart: many a senior scholar can produce a four-hundred-page study and yet be unable to generate a single-page summary of it that describes the work's intent and shape. Yet it's an excellent skill to have, and in a competitive publishing market it could make the difference between getting an editor's attention or not. Before you set out to turn your dissertation into a book manuscript, practice writing descriptions of your thesis. Forget about the dreary little dissertation abstract. Write a description with flesh on its bones and feeling behind the words. The map, the melodies, the throughline may reveal themselves as they have not before.

The beginning of a manuscript is the author's chance to seize the reader's attention and establish her authority as a guide. Whether a book opens with fireworks or a fistful of slowly cohering details, the first clutch of pages establishes terrain and the cartographer's skill. I like to invoke the Fifty-Page Rule: make your first fifty pages as perfect as you can make them. One of the ways you do this, especially in a revised dissertation, is by making clear that there is something at stake—something much more than your being awarded your doctoral degree. A clear structure says something important about your writing. "The book about to unfold will have a shape and a purpose, its reader will be repaid for the time she invests in the journey, and the author knows both the goal and the best way to reach it." Backpacks and walking sticks ready, everyone.

It may sound trivial to talk about subheads and length of paragraphs, but these are the building blocks of a book's map. The reader of a scholarly book is, in one important sense, no different from the reader of trade nonfiction. Each needs to be confident that the author-guide knows his way into the forest and out again. An editor wants to find a manuscript that is laid out in sections that are of a manageable length, in part because that will make the project more attractive to a reader. A manuscript that gives the appearance—*however superficial*—of having been thoughtfully organized will give the impression that it is thoughtful in other ways, too. In other words, a manuscript that looks like six great slabs of prose is probably just that. However complex the analyses within those slabs, an editor is likely to see the manuscript as heavy weather.

Subheads to the Rescue

Writers in command of their material and gifted at sustaining a narrative line—"natural writers," they are sometimes erroneously called—seem to be able simply to write the paragraph, and then the next and the next, until the chapter is complete. Most beginning scholars, though, face in the dissertation the longest piece of writing they have yet attempted—or attempted to revise. They need guides as much as their potential readers do. An easy way to create the inner map is through subheads, which break the text of a chapter into smaller sections, sometimes even into mere mouthfuls.

Subheads are a boon to the scholarly writer. With them, you can signal that you are taking on several discrete but connected points within the larger unit of the chapter. (You can also use the subheads to paper over at least some of the discontinuities in your writing. If you do this too obviously, however, an attentive reader will feel cheated.) In some disciplines, subheads are a common feature of scholarly writing. In other fields, they appear less frequently. For anyone revising a dissertation and uncertain whether the prose structure will stand on its own, I say go ahead and try breaking the writing into chunks and labeling them. You may like what results. Even if you don't, the effort may give you a clearer perspective on what you've been writing, and why you're having problems making it all fit together.

Sections within a chapter might be of any length. What's important is that each section—even if it is only a page long—has an internal coherence that justifies your setting it off. Sprinkling subtitles through poorly organized prose won't help.

Making a Table of Contents Work

Replacing the dissertation's title might be the best-known revision trick. But the most satisfying might be throwing out the table of contents and starting over. The average dissertation's contents page is a useless document. By now it is all too familiar: an introduction, perhaps a review of the literature, a gnomic listing of a half-dozen complex and specialized chapter titles that may or may not cohere, notes, and bibliography. Earnest but cryptic, the contents page seems innocent of its duty to point the reader through the text ahead.

You can fix your dissertation's table of contents, however, by opening it up so that it tells much more about what is happening within the book. And if done right, the rewrite of the table of contents will get you to rethink what goes on in the text itself. It's not unusual for this sort of revision to send the author weaving back and forth from table of contents to body text and back again.

Here is an example of a table of contents that goes through a couple of revisions. In the case of a dissertation entitled *Homeopathy in America: 1697–1789,* the title isn't really the problem. But once into the table of contents, the whole appears weakly conceived as a book (figure 1).

This table of contents may list exactly what the author has typed out at the head of each chapter, but when brought together the entries become an incoherent jumble of mismatches. It's not a lost cause, however. The title of the work—*Homeopathy in America*—is lucid, and the subtitle—*1697–1789*—clearly delineates the work's span. What happens next, however, could make sense only to the author and dissertation committee. The introduction sounds interesting, but an editor's interest is dashed by the appearance of "review of the literature" (which has no place in a published book, however necessary it may be as part of a dissertation manuscript). Chapter 3 is suddenly alert: the author has decorated it with a period quotation, and then identified her subject, wonderworking Molly Crenshaw, ministering angel of eighteenth-century New England. For the first time, a reader of the table of contents will feel that the author is interested in what she's writing. And that feeling disappears as the same reader eyes chapter 4. "Conflict and Consensus" might appear in just about any dissertation written on any subject by anyone ever. It might mean something like "the subject becomes quite complex here, and I've sorted it as best I can"—or not. As sympathetic as an editor might be to the writer's dilemma, it's a poor—and unrevealing—choice.

Chapter 5 is a puzzle. "Rhubarb"? A history of the plant and its medicinal uses? Could be interesting. Chapter 6: "A Time of

Contents

Acknowledgments		7
Chapter One	Introduction: "A frenzie for herbes" and the Construction of the Colonial Self	11
Chapter Two	Review of the Literature	63
Chapter Three	"What is this foul-smelling weed?": Molly Crenshaw and the Connecticut Valley Incurables	90
Chapter Four	Conflict and Consensus	149
Chapter Five	Rhubarb	188
Chapter Six	A Time of Transition	241
Notes		275
Bibliography		391

Figure 1. Sample table of contents, before revision

Transition." Not interesting. Like "Conflict and Consensus," this is a title that could be inserted into almost any doctoral thesis. (Try this: think of a period in which there was absolutely no transition whatsoever.) "Conflict and Consensus" and "A Time of Transition" are dull academic commonplaces, verbal Band-Aids where writers need something clear and descriptive or fresh and edgy. Figure 2 shows one solution to repairing this particular table of contents.

All that's happened in this iteration of the table of contents

Contents

Acknowledgments	~~7~~
Chapter One. Introduction: "A frenzie for herbes" and the Construction of the Colonial Self, 1697–1728	~~11~~
~~Chapter Two. Review of the literature~~	~~63~~
Chapter ~~Three.~~ Two. "What is this foul-smelling weed?": Molly Crenshaw and the Connecticut Valley Incurables, 1735–1737	63
Chapter ~~Four.~~ Three. The Cultivation of Simples and the Resistance to Their Use in Virginia and the Carolinas, 1720–1750	122
Chapter ~~Five.~~ Four. The Baltimore Rhubarb Riot of 1753 and the Rise of Self-Medication in Maryland	161
Chapter ~~Six.~~ Five. The Decline of the "Herbal Gentry" and the First Steps toward the "New Science" of Pharmacology, 1750–1789	214
Notes	258
Bibliography	374

Figure 2. Sample table of contents, revised

is that the review of the literature has been tossed out, and each of the chapters has been groomed to indicate a chronological span and a subject. Perhaps *Homeopathy in America: 1697–1789* is, at last, only a series of connected essays. But if they are connected with sufficient care and persuasiveness, such a project might yet be publishable in book form. Even if only specialists in colonial history or American medicine would conceivably pick such a book up, this table of contents at least demonstrates that the writer has specific historical or analytical material to offer. The massive notes section of this book suggests that the writer has done a vast amount of research.

Yet even this table of contents makes it hard for a reader to see what the book contains. A dissertation committee knows, of course. They've read it. An editor hasn't, and might not. This version needs reworking, both to indicate more fully what lies within the book, and also to demonstrate the author's awareness of the need to give signals.

Let's give it another try. Our student of colonial homeopathy has written six chapters, and has now retitled them, evening out the bumpy diction and creating a sense of chronological progress. The units of time overlap a bit, but that can help to convince the reader that this is real historical research. Still, this is the table of contents for a monograph, with no evident ambitions to reach a larger audience. But suppose that the book is in fact richer in historical research? Potentially useful to students of gender and American politics? Race in the eighteenth-century Atlantic? If these are reasonable goals for the book, this author needs to create a table of contents that will let these virtues shine. Figure 3 shows a further revision.

Let's look at what we've done this time. Each chapter has been "exploded"; where there had been simply a chapter title, with or without an explanatory subtitle, there is now also a second level of heads, delineating the subsections of that chapter. While it might still be hard to piece all these suggestive phrases—and that's all chapter and section titles are—into a coherent project, now there's an impression of liveliness that was completely missing in the last iteration.

This exercise is, of course, completely invented. Molly Crenshaw, that brave soul, never existed. I don't know whether there ever was a cult of recreational purgatives in colonial Boston. But if the writer of this manuscript were able to present what she knows in a sufficiently lively manner—both in the table of contents and in the text itself—there might be a wider readership for a book that expanded our understanding of how colonial Americans used, enjoyed, and even abused the

Contents

Figure 3. Sample table of contents, revised again

herbs on which their medical treatment depended. An editor who spotted the possibility of such a readership might also light upon the presence of Benjamin Franklin in the last chapter and retitle the book something like *Mr. Franklin's Parsley*, yoking the authority and familiarity of Franklin to an object dangled mysteriously before us. Exploding the table of contents is, in the first instance, the author's job. Finding the potential to push the book out to its widest audience is what editors do best.

A good table of contents announces an organized mind at work.

Signposting the Text

Homeopathy in America, with its exploded table of contents, gives a fairly clear map of where the book will take the reader. It isn't necessary to have all those subheads built into the contents page, but it certainly lays out the territory. You can add further levels of subheads to your manuscript, too, so that the reader who turns to the subsection "Mr. Franklin Investigates" will encounter several smaller sections within that section, each neatly titled. Every subhead that appears in the table of contents must appear in the text itself, though the reverse is not necessary. When I was writing the book you're reading, I thought that the title, subtitle, and table of contents (with chapter titles only) were sufficiently descriptive, so unlike the author of *Homeopathy in America* I didn't add subheads to the contents page.

Subheads are an example of *signposting,* direct announcements that the writer will gather the next several pages or paragraphs under one umbrella. A long chapter can sometimes feel like being told a story, or a lot of stories one after another, by a speaker breathless with excitement. But slow the speaker down, pause between episodes, and suddenly the point of it all becomes clearer. One of the easiest ways to revise a long chapter is to identify its shifts of emphasis and create a break before each one. You can come up with signposting subheads for a chapter in an hour or less. Like notices on the highway—"Falling rock next 500 yards," "Scenic overlook," "Gas food lodging"—subheads tell the reader what to keep an eye out for.

Some writers on writing disapprove of signposting in the text, finding it unsubtle and a sign of weak writing. Many great writers of nonfiction write wonderful books without these textual aids. But for someone revising a dissertation, subheads can be a way to ensure that even a nodding reader will know where he is. Keep in mind that a subhead directs, but it also interrupts. Don't overdo it. In some social science dissertations, practically every paragraph has a title. The result looks like a series of index cards printed in sequence.

Title, subtitle, table of contents, subheads within the text. All work toward one big goal: making clear what a work is about and where it's heading, and showing that you are in control. Do this and you show that you are interested in your reader.

Portion Control

A word on chapter length. The key to weight loss, so the diet books say, is portion control. It can be a good mantra for scholarly writers, too. Many scholarly books, especially dissertations, are like meals that go on for too long and where all the portions are far too large. Chapters are the portions of your work. They need to be of manageable size. You may have revised your table of contents so that all sixteen subheads in chapter 2 are proudly displayed, but at eighty-five pages, the chapter is creaking under its weight.

There aren't any hard and fast rules for chapter length, or paragraph length, or even manuscript length. Many editors will tell you that a manuscript of 350 double-spaced pages has a much greater chance of being published than one that's 500 pages long. Chapters should be readable at one comfortable sitting. A paragraph should rarely be more than a page in length, and a careful writer will hear in the prose the shift of emphasis that requires one paragraph to end and another to begin.

Here are a few generalizations especially pertinent to revising dissertations:

- A fifty-page chapter is either wordy or built on shaky premises. Is it really more than one chapter? Is it so long because it is well-planned and complex or because the writer's point is not clear? It's easier to hide a weak argument in a garrulous chapter than in a short one.
- Chapters whose logic flows clearly from paragraph to paragraph are rare. Introducing subsections and subheads can give you some architectural help and give the reader a chance to come up for air.
- Chapters brutally cut in two will look like chapters brutally cut in two. When revising an exceptionally long piece of writing, such as a ninety-page stretch of prose, be sure to shape both resulting pieces. The rules of opening and closing apply to both halves.

Last Looks

A lot of things happen to your manuscript once a publishing house has accepted it. Editors, designers, copy editors, and proofreaders all have a hand in helping you clarify what you have to say. To describe those varied functions would go well beyond the scope of this book. When your book is finally accepted, it's comforting to know that these professionals are on the other end and committed to helping you make your book its best. But knowing that these folks are out there, waiting for you beyond a publisher's reception desk, mustn't become an excuse not to make your book as strong and as clear as possible even while it's brewing at your desk. Editors and their colleagues are in the business of making good books even better. Never let that become an excuse for not putting your book into its best possible shape before you let it out of your hands.

In producing your first book manuscript, you need to check that your writing is well mapped, that a reader can find her way around from title page to conclusion. When your book is accepted, edited, and sent for typesetting, it will gain a new set of mapping features. Running heads—the text that stretches across the tops of the text pages—will help the reader know immediately which part or chapter of the book she is in. Some elaborately edited books may have running heads that change to reflect subheads in the text below. Your publisher's choice of font, decisions about how many lines to put on the page, where the notes should go, and so on will all affect the clarity with which your ideas present themselves. We take these ordinary details for granted, but they too are tools with which a reader comes to know what's inside your head.

The last mapping your book provides is the index. In some complicated books there may be two or more indexes, as for example, an index of concepts and an index of place names. Think of an index as the author's last chance to tell a story about the work she has just completed. *Library Journal,* to name one book review periodical on which librarians depend for information, will usually note whether or not a book has an index. If your work is scholarly, an index is crucial. A good index is a treasure, and though it isn't something you can prepare before your revised manuscript is accepted by a publishing house and set into proof, it's worth pointing out that there are good indexes and poor ones. The minimalist index gets away with including only proper names, and indeed this is the easiest type of index entry to create. Such is this example from the helpful monograph *Reference Publishing as Depicted in Hollywood Cinema:*

> Stanwyck, Barbara, 5–6, 18, 37, 44, 111, 158–60, 350n

The same entry might have been conceived more usefully by breaking it down into subcategories.

> Stanwyck, Barbara: *Ball of Fire,* depictions of editors in, 5–6, 18, 37; cross-references, dispute with Gary Cooper concerning, 158; Dewey, Melvil, unrequited passion for, 159; encyclopedias, attitude toward in childhood, 44; *The Lady Eve,* dependency on pocket dictionary during filming of, 111, 350n; and serial commas, 160

It's considerably more difficult to create an index that includes abstract concepts, but the more extensive and thoughtful an index is, the more useful to the reader. Like the title and subtitle, the table of contents, and the forte and piano alterations of big and small subheads, the index is one final opportunity to elucidate what the book wants to say.

Writing—even scholarly writing—needs shape, and shape comes about in many ways. If you're already good at imposing shape in your writing, you possess a skill that can set you above other writers who might have tackled grander ideas in their manuscripts. This focus on mapping your text is meant to help you create a manuscript that looks reader-friendly because it is reader-friendly. A book-length manuscript needs to be more than three hundred nicely written pages. It's got to have markers for your reader, so that he knows where he is and where you want to take him. In writing your book, be sure that all roads lead to home. Shaping title, subtitle, chapters, sections, subsections, and paragraphs takes patience, attention, a good ear. Finally—and this is one editor's view—if you can write one terrific paragraph, you have it in you to write an entire book.

8

Making Prose Speak

It's time to say something about writing itself. Different kinds of books are written for different audiences, and dissertations are, of course, most often revised to turn them into serious scholarly books. Sometimes the author has an ambition to turn the dissertation into something for scholars and a slightly broader, nonuniversity readership. Some few authors will aim to turn the dissertation into a book that could sit in a tall stack near the checkout at Barnes & Noble. The broader the audience you seek, the more carefully an editor will scrutinize your writing. Aim for "anyone interested in childhood" and you'll need to have a mighty engaging prose style (as well as something astonishingly fresh to say). Aim for "anyone interested in the manufacture of children's toys in nineteenth-century America" and you can assume a more determined readership, but you still need to write well. A cynic might conclude that, following this logic, the readership for one's dissertation is so small that the prose style hardly counts at all. But that's giving in to self-pity. Remember that in the first and most important instance, you write to find out what you think. The more clearly you write, the more clearly you are thinking. And if that doesn't matter to you, you're in the wrong line of work. In revising, your first task is to rescue your ideas from "dissertation style."

"Dissertation Style"

"Dissertation style" is a kind of awful description of writing, since it seems to be used only as a term of disparagement. The kind of style a dissertation might have is the kind of style you wouldn't want for, say, your clothes or your car. Dissertation style connotes a lot things:

- An overdependence on citation and reference
- An effortful attempt to sound very professional, which comes out sounding stuffy
- Repetitious statements of intent ("I am going to analyze three elements of X," "I have now analyzed one element of X and will now analyze the second before continuing to the third," "Thus have I demonstrated through my analyses of the three elements of X" and so on)
- An overuse of passives and elaborate syntactic constructions
- Either an unseemly pompousness or a willed lifelessness, as if being a professional scholar meant showing as little expression as possible (and sometimes a dissertation manages to exhibit both).

Bad dissertation writing inevitably reminds me of the sort of play in which young actors in gray wigs and heavy makeup play characters forty years older. The plays might be comedies and the effect intentional, but the dissertation is deadly serious, all awkward striving to prove that the writer is indeed a professional scholar and grown up at last. Few of the very best professional scholars, the ones we read for pleasure as well as knowledge, write the way dissertations read, and scholarly editors often wonder why the best academic books can't be models for the rising generation of Ph.D.'s. Instead, the average dissertation takes what seems to be the path of least resistance, replicating an inert prose style that sounds very much like the inert prose style of thousands of dissertations that have gone before. It need not be so.

You won't be able to transform a dissertation into a book manuscript without looking at your writing voice. Everyone knows what a writing voice is in fiction. Jane Austen sounds different from Salman Rushdie. Dissertations might be voiceless, or feel that way. Actually, they aren't voiceless, even if the writer feels that way. But every *book* has to have a narrative voice that draws the reader in, revealing perspectives and tastes connected to the topic under discussion. The phrase "talking book" is often used to describe audio versions of printed text. But every book is *already* a talking book. You need to make yours one, too.

Publishers will likely pay more attention to your prose than did your dissertation committee, because publishers are looking for something beyond your qualifications to write on the subject. And however good your research may be, it's your writing that makes the first impression. If the impression is poor, it may be your last as well.

It is a fact of scholarly life that many important books are hard to read. Badly written, if you like. Others are not really badly written, but are unforgivingly dense. In all fairness, many of these books, and perhaps most, are written as well and as clearly as the author could manage. It's too easy for a new writer to find a published book and use it to justify writing her own manuscript in clunky prose.

Some disciplines are more tolerant of dense writing than are others, but almost all readers outside these disciplines are critical of academic prose. When books by the intellectual elite are written in forbidding language, graduate students are understandably encouraged to believe that this is the argot in which they must write, too. Some powerful thinkers write in terribly difficult prose, but it becomes a disservice to the academic community when complex writing is presented as the norm, even an obligation.

If ideas and presentation must be put into relative importance, most editors will tacitly agree that if you're *that smart* the quirks and difficulties of your writing won't matter. If you're not yet writing at that level, or haven't yet achieved that celebrity, make clarity your god. While you're polishing your prose, imagine what Adorno or Lacan might have said if they had been graced with the gift of direct and easy expression. Clear writing shows off ideas best. Jewels can hide in thickets of difficult prose, but the writer of a first book should think in terms of clarity, clarity, clarity.

The problems that afflict dissertation prose are *always* equally problematic in a book manuscript, and usually more so. Vague, overlong constructions, for example, that meander down the page until they run out of steam or stumble into a block quotation. But beyond this sort of weakness there are other writing flaws.

Pronoun Trouble

Now a word about the obscuring, commanding, cajoling, imperial We.

Poor Queen Victoria has taken a lot of ribbing. I don't know if she really used the Royal We as often as popular culture suggests, but it's certain that academic writers—who would cringe at the suggestion they were being Victorian—are addicted to the first-person plural. For some reason, the writer of the dissertation rarely seems to be doing things alone. Many graduate students have been made to feel uncomfortable with "I." It's too naked or too cheeky for a beginner. How much nicer to be we. Suddenly, the writer isn't alone. There's a crowd investigating scansion in Tennyson's *In Memoriam* or the efficiency of paper ballots in Honduran elections. A therapist might identify a self-esteem issue here: who is this imaginary entourage? What special friend helped you write your dissertation and goes uncredited on the title page?

Academia doesn't seem ready to send its troops out from behind "we," and it's just pragmatic to acknowledge that "we" isn't going to disappear soon as the pronoun of academic choice. But from the perspective of an editor advising recent Ph.D.'s and doctoral students how to make a dissertation sound like a book (and how it sounds is part of the battle), "we" is a problem. If you've written a dissertation collectively, each of the authors might be entitled to "we." Beyond that, "we" has little justification. The skillful writer uses a more neutral voice. In some cases, the writer presents himself nakedly as "I," though this can be just as wearisome as "we." In the best academic writing, the author's persona is present through the choice of language and the clarity of argument, but not through assertive pronouns. Let your facts or your interpretation speak.

"As we have seen," begins the dissertation, and so I find myself looking around quickly to see who is peering over my shoulder. The imaginary collective reader is a commonplace of scholarly writing. Thousands of dissertations, as well as scholarly articles and monographs, appeal to the slippery "we." Is the writer using an intimate "we"—just herself-as-writer and me-as-her-reader? Perhaps her "we" is more crowded, a pack of like-minded scholars at which she is, however modestly, at the vanguard? Or is the "we" meant to write me, too, into this larger scholarly community? I might be flattered that the writer thinks I'm smart enough to join in, but as a reader I don't much like being told what I think.

Suggest to a doctoral candidate that she use the pronoun "I" instead and you're likely to encounter embarrassed resistance. "That's not the way it's done in my field." "The dissertation must sound professional, and this is how it's done by professionals." "Thanks for the advice—but, sorry, we couldn't." Professional standards and rules aren't made by individual doctoral advisors, any more than a single graduate student can decide to ignore a writing practice accepted in her discipline.

Dissertations are commonly written in one of three narrative modes: we, I, and (invisible). The first two acknowledge the presence of the writer. The third stages every sentence without reference to the writer, employing what I came to know in grade school as the "omniscient narrator." The irony of this third option can be painful, as dissertation writers are among the least likely people to feel omniscient about anything. When revising a dissertation into a book manuscript, think about the perspective from which the story unfolds. Anyone picking up your book will know from the opening pages just where the writer stands in relation to his text. If you're planning to revise your dissertation into a book for a general as opposed to a specialized scholarly readership, this issue is more acute still. No trade book will succeed with an uncertain narrative voice.

The "we" problem is closely related to the "passive" problem. In both cases, the scholar is looking for a perspective from which to write. It's like choosing the right clothes for a job interview. Will all black be too much? If I wear the blazer and tie will I blend in so well they'll think I already work there? Is the hat just asking for trouble? It isn't as if the writer of a dissertation sits down to write page 1 and dithers over a multitude of options. She will write with "I" or "we," or she will disappear down the passive. (It's unlikely anyone will be awarded a Ph.D. for a dissertation written in the second person present, which would make it sound like *The Twilight Zone:* "You are researching the cost of housing in Hong Kong when you discover a disturbing fact about drywall construction.")

So why have so many scholars become "we" on the page? Perhaps because the dynamics of academia tolerate only limited individuality, because the training of scholars remains in many ways a guild process, because one of the ways we have come to recognize formal discourse is through its use of the first-person plural. "We" isn't wrong or cowardly, not even in dissertations. But unless a dissertation was written by more than one person, or unless the author's thesis demands that appeals to universality occur in every sentence, there's no reason why the collective pronoun should be put in the driver's seat.

Doctoral students don't have a lot of time to worry about narrative voice, and not many dissertation advisors have time to work on it with their advisees. Revision for publication may be the first time the young scholar steps back to discover what voice is telling her story. Look at revision as the opportunity to find out who your writing self is.

Footnote Madness

The footnote, as Anthony Grafton puts it, has "a curious history" bound up with the rise of modern German historiography. Medieval academic debate took place under a different sun, where Aristotle was so great his name had no need to be mentioned. *Ipse dixit*—"he said"—was enough for a reader to know who "he" was. We moderns have invented more elaborate systems for borrowing thoughts from others. Judging from the look of the unrevised dissertation, academic research appears to erode a scholar's confidence; it often seems to a publisher that nothing can be said without citing some authority. The date of the Battle of Gettysburg, the number of member states in the United Nations, the weight of an Atlantic cod—any fact seems to require a citation, as if common sense or common knowledge were not to be factored into the equation.

The first rule of scholarly writing is to acknowledge precisely all work and ideas that are not your own. Rightly so. But too many notes can be a distraction for the reader, and after a few hundred citations sometimes the writer gets lost in the forest. The problem of excess citation is a problem of dependency. For the writer of the dissertation it is more than a single problem. First, the average dissertation simply has too many notes, among which the author either deliberately hides or struggles in vain to break free. Second, the present system of notating every small thought vitiates the bigger ideas, which after all are the point of the book. Finally, many citations seem to do nothing more than embroider a well-known name into the fabric of one's thesis, whether or not that authority's work is apposite or even clearly understood by the young scholar.

Many ideas that have wide currency within the academy are big, difficult, and subtle. But some have been reduced to a sort of semaphore that suggests the user knows them thoroughly and has found an ingenious way to apply them to the work at hand. Judith Butler's work on gender. Clifford Geertz's reflections on Balinese cockfighting. Bakhtin's concept of the dialogic. Benjamin's insight into mechanical reproduction. Hegel's popular (and all-purpose) dialectic. From all of these, thousands of graduate students have pinched just enough seasoning to flavor their own soup. Publishers are weary of citations that merely nod at, rather than use, the well-established work of major scholars.

It isn't enough, then, merely to cite. But there are more problems with citation madness. Consider the physical appearance of the sentence. There is the superscript pointing to a footnote or endnote, in the *Chicago Manual of Style* manner, which if overused can make the dissertation page look carbonated.

> This argument[62] about Hobbema's late canvases[63] requires that we first examine the aforesaid pamphlet by Hobart[64] and a lecture on Hegel by Hildebrand,[65] first delivered in Havana.[66]

Turning to the practice of the social scientists, things get no better.

> This argument (Hundertwasser 1989, 65–72) about Hobbema's late canvases (House 1965, 188; Hoving 1988, 190–203; Havemeyer 1999, xi) requires that we first examine the aforesaid pamphlet by Hobbes (Harley 1988, 35–82) and a lecture by Hebworth (Heath 1991, 18–40), first delivered in Havana in 1983 (Hilton 1992, 36–60).

The reader knows she is in for a long, slow journey.

Each discipline has its particular conventions of citation. Besides the *Chicago Manual,* there is the *MLA* (Modern Language Association) *Stylesheet,* and the *APA* (American Psychological Association) *Stylesheet.* Sociologists, literary critics, and psychologists might each cite their sources in a different format. Beyond the citation style, there is a choice as to where the notes will be placed on the book page. Real footnotes go at the bottom (or foot) of the page. So-called chapter notes are gathered at the end of each chapter. Endnotes appear at the end of the book. If you're writing a book for a general reader, there are even ways of presenting your endnotes so that they don't require superscripts or other interruptions to the text page. A scholarly work, such as a revised dissertation will most likely be, needs superscripts. The only recourse for the young scholar is to avoid piling up references so densely that her sentences, like the examples above, look like multiple car wrecks.

If you're working in the social sciences or other disciplines where it has become acceptable to include brief citations within the text itself, remember that when scholars in these fields turn to writing trade books they leave this practice behind them. A specialist might want to know, in the middle of your carefully worded thought, that you are citing Elmwood 1998b, for the full details of which you then flip to the reference list. As a demonstration of your intellectual probity, a discreet superscript and footnote would do. Reading scholarly work would be more agreeable if Elmwood 1998b weren't considered an attractive way of proving one wasn't making it all up.

Citation madness has other perils. In the rush to demonstrate that she knows the literature, the young scholar quotes too frequently. Then she quotes at too great length. Sometimes—and this is the heartbreaking moment—she quotes too beautifully. Here is a passage by the food writer M. F. K. Fisher. It's most of the conclusion to her volume *How to Cook a Wolf,* published in 1942:

> Those few of us who actually live to eat are less repulsive than boring, and at this date I honestly know of only two such lost souls, gross puffy creatures, both of them, who are exhibited like any other monstrous curiosity by their well-fed but still balanced acquaintances.
>
> On the other hand, I cannot count the good people I know who, to my mind, would be even better if they bent their spirits to the study of their own hungers. There are too many of us, otherwise in proper focus, who feel an impatience for the demands of our bodies, and who try throughout our whole lives, none too successfully, to deafen ourselves to the voices of our various hungers. Some stuff the wax of religious solace in our ears. Others practice a Spartan if somewhat pretentious disinterest in the pleasures of the flesh, or pretend that if we do not admit our sensual delight in a ripe nectarine we are not guilty . . . of even that tiny lust!

I believe that one of the most dignified ways we are capable of, to assert and then reassert our dignity in the face of poverty and war's fears and pains, is to nourish ourselves with all possible skill, delicacy, and ever-increasing enjoyment. And with our gastronomical growth will come, inevitably, knowledge and perception of a hundred other things, but mainly of ourselves. Then Fate, even tangled as it is with cold wars and hot, cannot harm us.

It is difficult to compete with Fisher, whose feeling for food and for feeling itself radiates from the pages of her essays. To think about food, even the poorest food, in time of war, opens for her a path to enlightenment. Suddenly, anything—even an omelet—can be the means of increasing one's self-knowledge. Fisher's "knowledge and perception of a hundred other things" is what we read for, and what we write for, too. Substitute for Fisher an elegant or powerful writer in the discipline in which you are working and the result will be the same. Strong writers, like strong perfume, should be used with great care. Comparison with your own prose will be inevitable.

When reading a scholar's first book-length manuscript, I skip block quotations if they are already familiar. And many of them are. I don't need to read one more time a three-inch chunk of prose on the theory of the female gaze. If the film scholar Laura Mulvey's work has been important to your own thinking, as it may well be if you are in cinema studies, make that clear. But absorb these well-read passages. Naturalize them within your prose.

Some scholars have pointed out to me that block quotations are the parts of a book, or dissertation, that they skip anyway, so what you put in them doesn't much matter. This is a depressing thought, and if true it means that quoting prose far better than one's own is at least not a dangerous move. Better, I think, to interpret this perspective as a further encouragement not to take up space, and lose the reader's attention, with generous servings of prose from the already published.

One Example Too Many

Dissertations talk too much. Don't feel bad—most books do, and not just scholarly books. I've mentioned earlier what every editor knows: that dissertations are characteristically shaped around a set of examples meant to demonstrate an argument or at least to work through a set of concerns. But too many examples can also mar academic prose within a single chapter. As you reread your work, be ruthless in revising any paragraph that begins, optimistically enough, "This point will be further clarified by an additional example," or words to that effect. There are many instances when a point is best made by one trenchant example rather than by four fuzzy ones.

Dissertation revision—and let me make my plea again that you think of the task as bespoke tailoring, not just fixing the hem—works best when the writer sees a core idea and a throughline, and then cuts everything that doesn't help her express both. You may still need to write more in order to make the manuscript talk like a book, but cutting back anything written on academic autopilot is a step in the right direction.

Passive Is Spoken Here

The hallmark of academic writing is the passive voice. Most writing guides are vigilantes on the lookout for stray passives. "Whenever you come across a passive in your writing, recast the sentence with an active verb instead." The examples tend to feature painful structures and why-didn't-I-think-of-that transformations. "When the book had been read by the class, the next lesson was presented by the teacher" becomes "When the students had read the book the teacher presented the lesson." Yet it's difficult to convince academic writers that avoiding the passive is a piece of advice meant for *them.*

In weak academic writing, passives abound. (I might have said "passives are frequently used" but I wanted an active verb here.) If you were reading a poorly written letter or a grade school composition, you might think that the writer simply didn't have sufficient command to write in direct and vivid terms. He might even have been aware of his limitations, embarrassed by the idea of expressing his opinion in a naked way, and taking refuge behind the curtain of the passive.

By the time a writer is toiling on the dissertation, his printer has spit out a lot of term papers. His unlearned writing lessons have now become his writing habits. Those habits, in turn, have become his characteristic way of expressing ideas. He has grown used to—even fond of—them. (I find it unsurprisingly easy to view the weaknesses in my own writing as being part of my style.) Years of abusing the passive have encouraged the advanced graduate student to believe that the passive is, after all, the voice of academia. If this is how the scholarly world speaks—or rather, if this is the language spoken in the scholarly world—then there can be no better time to deploy it than in writing the dissertation.

The passive voice does two things at once—concealing the author while claiming authority—and those two things at first seem contradictory. It's easy to see how the passive conceals agency, or responsibility for action. "The overthrow of the country's tottering regime was undertaken by the forces of the Army of Liberation in the late spring of 1963." Let's let that army take responsibility for its actions: "Late in the spring of 1963 the Army of Liberation overthrew the country's tottering regime." Suddenly, the Army of Liberation did it.

There's another concealment at work here, too. The passive construction distances the writer from the act of making a statement. Take away the passive, and the writer—like the Army of Liberation—has suddenly done something of consequence: he's made a declaration. He's said something. You don't have to be an expert in linguistics to know that this is not the same thing as "something was said." But too many dissertations are written in an imaginary world where objects have things done to them and countries are invaded, characters are depicted, and results are secured. It's not that the passive is a criminal offense for writers. There are plenty of places where passive constructions feel right. Use them there. Prose stripped entirely of passives can feel overly energetic, like a kindergarten class at recess. "Calm down!" you want to say. But hyperkinetic prose isn't a writing problem that afflicts dissertations, and so I'm going to ignore it here. I think it helps to draw a distinction between writing *with* the passive voice and writing *in* the passive voice.

In the first case, the writer uses the passive when it's necessary. In control of her prose, she enjoys the way the passive voice lends variety to her sentences, yet she remains the boss in her own paragraphs. On the other hand, someone who writes *in the passive* hopes no one will notice that she's there. The passive is a cozy place to hide. Writing can be like going through customs. "Anything to declare?" asks a flint-eyed customs officer. Most people rely on a cheerful smile and a shake of the head, hoping there won't be any questions about the extra bottle of wine or the embroidered tablecloth. Most academic writing hopes to slither through customs, too. Instead of a smile, scholarly writers too often depend on the passive, fearful that a direct statement might open them to equally direct inspection.

But the passive voice is also about authority. It's an authority based not on accumulated research or the wisdom of experience, at least not in the case of most dissertations, but on an appeal to the power of passivity. In this sense, the passive is the first cousin of the imperial We.

To use the passive is to call up the authority of one's discipline and the scholars who have gone before. There's nothing wrong with wanting to do this, but the passive can't get you there all by itself. Academic writers—particularly young academic writers—use the passive to lend credibility to their writing. "Domestic arrangements in sixteenth-century Lancashire households were often made by the eldest daughter." Domestic arrangements are in charge of this sentence, while the writer's point appears to be that the eldest daughter of the household looked after things. In its Olympian calm, the passive asserts—even demands—that the reader agree. Nevertheless, this sentence is nervous about its own claims, as the tell-tale word "often" makes clear. Was the eldest daughter in charge or wasn't she? Is the writer making an important and original claim about family relationships or just serving up someone else's research nugget? If it's an original idea, it's too compressed to be clear, too wimpy to be convincing. A bit better: "My research reveals the surprising fact that the eldest daughter was responsible for domestic arrangements in most sixteenth-century Lancashire households." ("Most" is quantitative and useful here; "often" is a fudge.) If it's someone else's thought and worth paraphrasing, the point needs sharpening. "As Henry Pismire has pointed out, in almost half the sixteenth-century Lancashire households for which we have records, the eldest daughter was responsible for domestic arrangements.[23]" Better because clearer.

It's critical for young scholars to understand that all this bother about the passive voice isn't simply a matter of making sentences lively, peppy, more engaging. Yes, the active voice is stronger. Readers listen more attentively because they can hear another human trying to engage their attention. But for scholars, the active-passive conundrum should be so much more. The active voice says, "I have something to say and I'm going to say it. If I'm wrong, argue with me in print. But take me at my worth." The active voice should be a kind of scholarly credo: I did research, I drew conclusions, I found this out. That's rarely what we get. How much more often do we read that research is conducted, conclusions are drawn, findings are found? I sometimes imagine a scholar sitting down with a great idea, then staring at his laptop and exclaiming "Are you crazy? You can't say that—" and clicking the toolbar to call up Active-Voice-Replace, instantly turning every "I found" into "It was discovered."

Dickens opens *David Copperfield* with a question that arrests me each time I come across it. "Whether I shall turn out to be the hero of my own life, or whether that station will be held by anybody else, these pages must show." He even uses a passive. *All writing—even the dissertation—is always about the writer.* Even in scholarly work, a writer is very much present, more subtly than in Nabokov or Beckett, perhaps, but present nonetheless. Every dissertation writer should strive to be the hero of her or his own work, taking command not only of the details but of the voice that presents them, knowing when to appear and when to step aside, how to attract the reader's attention and how to deflect it. In doing so, the scholarly writer becomes responsible for what "these pages must show," a world of causality and motivation where arguments are logical and evidence is clearly presented, a world where nouns noun and verbs verb.

Some passives we're glad we haven't had to see:

- In the beginning the heavens and the earth were created by God.
- Arms and the man are being sung by me.
- Ishmael is what I'm called.

The passive is a buffer, not only between the reader and the writer, but between the writer and her own ideas. I wonder if anyone experiences the world as a series of passive engagements. ("Yesterday, as the garden path was being trod by my feet, a beautiful butterfly was seen by my eye." Which sounds like a case for Dr. Oliver Sacks.) Academic writing often places the reader in just such a world, one where no feet cross any paths, no eye sees any butterfly. If your dissertation was worth writing, it's because you found a path you had to follow, and on the way you came upon something you want to tell others about. Do that.

The Point of Punctuation

The redoubtable Webster instructs us that the colon is "a punctuation mark : used chiefly to direct the attention to matter (as a list, explanation, quotation, or amplification) that follows." The colon has also insinuated its way into scholarly prose as a signal for unexpected connection. But the semicolon is the blue security blanket of academic writing. It was long my favorite punctuation mark, though I admit we don't really need it. The Big Five—the period, the comma, the question mark, the exclamation, and the quotation mark—could get the work done. But when you're a child one of the ways you know you're growing up is by discovering that the semicolon and the colon are tools that you, just like published writers, can use to communicate.

I guess many people have grown up with the sense that the colon and semicolon are the adult punctuation marks. Colons and semicolons, however, are take-charge types. They need to be watched.

There are, of course, plenty of situations where the colon can be used with a clear conscience. It can introduce lists, a quotation, and so on. That's not where a writer gets into trouble. Problems arise when you use the colon as if it were a conjunction. Take this example:

> The theoretical model articulated by Foucault is challenged by the work of a growing body of scholars: the panopticon is an insufficient metaphor through which to examine the relation of the individual to the matrix of social controls that support, restrain, and also define the self.

Why is there a colon here? Replace it with a period and you have two independent sentences. Replace it with the words "who regard" [the panopticon as] and the sentence is wordy but clear. There are scholars, the writer argues, who have grown tired of Foucault's panopticon because it no longer speaks to their perceptions of group-individual relations.

The writer has used a colon to make the sentence sound more complex. "Here is order," the colon purrs. "Here is balance." The colon is the fulcrum. (I could have written "Here is order, here is balance: the colon is the fulcrum.") Where a long sentence would connect each of the pieces together and make clear the agent (some scholars), the colon interrupts. In place of a wordy, long sentence the writer has created a stylish break and offered a moment of visual pleasure. Poets know best the rules and pleasures of punctuation and rhythm, but this isn't a matter to be left in their hands only. Somewhere along the line, it seems that everyone learns to deploy the colon as a way of heightening the mystery in a sentence, presenting two clauses but erasing the logical connection as if to say "You and I know how these two clauses relate to one another. Let's listen to them resonate and enjoy the pleasure in not having the connection spelled out." For academic writers, the lure of implied meaning is irresistible, and the colon is the visual marker of implied connection. The writer feels smarter for using the colon, and the reader enjoys the pleasure of a text that looks smart even before its messages are unpacked.

Some writers are addicted to the colon as conjunction. But the colon shouldn't be used this way. Your prose isn't richer for it, and you don't look smarter. Use the colon for lists, for ratios, and when you want to make an infrequent special effect.

Music, or the rhythm of your writing, is something we don't talk about much (unless we're taking creative writing classes, I suppose, and then we're not writing dissertations). But we all feel it as we do it. It's what makes us happy about the shape of a sentence, the shuttling between long and short phrases, the alternation of big and little words, the repetition of sounds. The most sturdily unpoetical writer can take pleasure in what he's written not merely for its data or its models but for the way the sentences sound to him when he reads them aloud.

The colon is formal. What the colon does in black tie, the semicolon does in khakis. Most people own more tan slacks than dinner jackets, and just so the semicolon enjoys more frequent appearances in sentences. It's difficult to imagine writing—and especially academic writing—without that dot-capped comma. Remember all the signals a colon radiates— "Pay special attention here!" "Watch this space!" "Guess how the pieces fit together!" You'll find them all here again with the semicolon, only this time in a lower key. A sentence will go about doing its business until it reaches the brick wall of the period, or the gap in the bridge that a colon makes the reader jump, or the little wall of the semicolon over which the reader must clamber. Academic writers love nothing more than these little walls; they create the feeling of subtle connection between parts of a sentence, even when the writer could have made the connection clearer or broken the sentence in two. The sentence you've just read didn't need a semicolon, but I liked the music of it and the way it asked you not to let your attention flag quite yet.

The semicolon is the scholar's favorite punctuation mark. Joseph Mitchell, the *New Yorker* writer who was famous for sitting in his office year after year without producing a single essay, nevertheless churned out several volumes of reportage in his younger days. As a newspaper man in the 1920s he had to cover the career of Nicholas Murray Butler, longtime president of Columbia University. Mitchell didn't like him much. "Even the semicolons are pompous on Nicholas Murray Butler's mimeographed statements," he wrote in a 1938 essay called "My Ears Are Bent," complaining that the adoring American press seemed not to notice. Here he is in characteristic form, talking about the frustrations of being a reporter:

> When a city editor catches you looking cross-eyed at your notes and wishing black plagues on the head of the inarticulate lulu you have just interviewed he is sometimes nice enough to put you on the street for a while, or on rewrite, or maybe a big story breaks and saves your sanity. Just when you are about to collapse with one of the occupational diseases of the reporter—indigestion, alcoholism, cynicism and Nicholas Murray Butler are a few of them—a big story, a blood-hunt that takes you out of the office, usually breaks.

The diction, the pacing, the sauce between the dashes make this passage work. Note the absence of colons or semicolons. Butler may have been pompous, but semicolons helped him get there. If you're not careful, they will take you to the same place, too. Most academics use semicolons far too often.

Two kinds of semicolon misuse commonly appear in academic writing. In both the writer imposes connections that aren't quite earned. The Grappling Hook Effect is one. Sometimes writing gets out of hand. Sentences feature elaborate constructions, and as those sentences expand and develop, their writer finds herself in need of a way to hang all this information and reflection on a suitable armature. The semicolon seems the natural tool. The resulting sentences are often far too long and are asked to do too much work.

> The revolution in ideas that we know as the Enlightenment affected the lives of individuals at all levels of society, including those who were unaware that there had been a social contract all along, even though they themselves had never signed it; the French perception of the relationship of highest to lowest in a world no longer dominated by the Church and the obfuscating mythologies that lingered on during the endless death of medieval thought that some experienced as the Renaissance is exemplified by the fate of the peasant we know only as Squinty in the town of Puits-sur-Loire.

Squinty's story may turn out to be one of those marvelous tales recovered by a lucky scholar with a good eye. But this sentence needs help. The semicolon seems to be there only to suture the big generalization in the first half of the sentence to the breathless second half. There's too much after the semicolon. The writer packs in (a) French Enlightenment views of society; (b) a distracting aside about the persistence of medievalism throughout the Renaissance; and (c) the surprise appearance of a character and place about which we might want to know more. The second, impossible part of this sentence cries out for a red pencil.

> The revolution in ideas that we know as the Enlightenment affected the lives of individuals at all levels of society, whether they knew it or not. ~~including those who were unaware that there hade been a social contract all along, even though they themselves had never signed it;~~ The French perception of the relationship of highest to lowest in a world no longer dominated by the Church ~~and the obfuscating mythologies that lingered on during the endless death of medieval thought that some experienced as the Renais-~~

sance ~~is exemplified by the fate of the peasant we know only~~ as Squinty in the town of Puits-sur-Loire.

All right, there's a passive here. But this is a big improvement.

Evil partner of the Grappling Hook Effect is the Implicit Connection Effect. The second misuse of the semicolon is more complex, and more difficult to repair. It is to writing what eye-contact avoidance is to conversation. Here the writer has several things to say, but is hesitant to press them to a conclusion. Implications are many, conclusions few.

This isn't the same as nuanced writing, where the author has something to say and goes about doing it with both precision and delicate shadings. Proust could wield a mean semicolon. There are eight in the first paragraph of *A la recherche du temps perdu,* and I wouldn't touch a single one. Scholars, though, need to subject the semicolon to a more rigorous discipline.

Here is an example of a piece of research prose in which the writer lets the semicolon stick each separate statement onto the one alongside it.

The organization of village life in Puits-sur-Loire has been characterized as "representative of its period and region,"[37] "difficult to describe based on the available data,"[38] and "brimming with activity";[39] those members of the village unable to read or, on the basis of court records, only intermittently employed, would still likely be active participants in seasonal festivals, including the little-known Fête des Potirons,[40] mentioned only once in the documents, yet central to the events of this narrative; among the village "characters" whose identities have come down to us, the itinerant mushroom gatherer we know as Squinty would likely have been in attendance at the lively fête, his mushrooms added to the communal stew;[50] all that winter, however, the handful of surviving villagers must surely have wondered what had suddenly killed so many on that crisp October day; at this point, regrettably, Squinty disappears from the archive.

The paragraph is a tissue of speculations and generalities, out of which the writer hopes to draw a series of causal relationships that would explain the fatalities in an eighteenth-century French village. This time a red pencil won't be of much help. There isn't much argument here, much less evidence. In their place we have the semicolon.

These elements of style show up in almost every scholar's writing at one time or another. The goal shouldn't be to expunge them from your prose. There is room for the well-placed passive and the adroitly wielded semicolon. Room, too, for a "we," as long as it doesn't wax grandiloquent or hide the speaker's identity under a paper bag. But as you revise your thesis, keep an eye out and an ear open. Whatever feels like a weakness in the writing of a dissertation will be even more evident if it persists into the book manuscript. Not far down the road the pebble in the shoe will feel like a boulder.

Good writing involves a kind of mystery of physics. As the author, you stand between the two things you want to reach out and touch, your subject and your reader. The odd thing about fixing wonky clauses and fugitive pronouns and superfluous annotation is that the better at it you become, the closer you get to both of your objectives. You grow closer to your reader because you're easier to understand, and then, wonderfully, you grow closer to your subject—you understand it better—because as your writing clears, you get to know what you think. You want your prose to speak not only to your unseen readers, but to yourself as well.

9

What Happens Next

At the beginning of Thomas Mann's novel *Buddenbrooks,* a child is listening to a story. "What happens next?" she asks, and the answer to the question becomes the novel. As it is a novel about several generations of a family, the answer will tell the child who she is, where she has come from, and where life is about to take them. What-happens-next is what stories are about. It is, less grandly, what all kinds of writing require. Writing a dissertation feels nothing like writing a novel. But dissertations are genuine acts of writing nonetheless, subject to many of the same requirements as a work of fiction. As you revise your work, taking it from one stage to another, don't lose sight of the forward drive. Like an old-fashioned novel, a dissertation has its own version of what-happens-next, but reveals it through arguments and evidence, examples that build, and a final stop in which some sort of closure is offered as the last pleasure of reading.

Think clearly. Create structures that engage and sustain interest across that great stretch of time during which you expect to hold your reader captive. Let your insights and imagination fill the sails of your craft.

The Curriculum Vitae and the Vita Nuova

A scholar's life is a writing life. In some fields, like the sciences, that writing may consist of a handful of carefully researched articles, published in peer-review journals with nary a thought of a book. In some disciplines the book is disdained, and the idea of publishing one's dissertation is simply not part of the equation. Mathematicians don't rush to pop the newly approved dissertation into the mail. But the humanities and social sciences view the world differently: their tools aren't labs or equations, but language, and their faculties are expected to write.

The life of scholarship is, as the social sciences have taught us to say, deeply contested. It can be lonely, grinding work into which lives disappear. You can awake one morning from uneasy dreams to find that you have been transformed into a professor, a curious anomaly within a society impatient with intellectual problems and what appear to be the narcissistic battles within the academic community. If you are fortunate, you will be granted tenure, thereby marrying your colleagues. Great teachers are possessed of a great gift. You may be one of those, and that may be a source of deep pleasure in your professional life. But all scholars have in common a commitment to the workings of the mind and to the dissection of argument, to the recovery of hidden truth and the dissemination of knowledge. To do that, you must write, and go on writing.

A scholar is a professional writer of high-protein nonfiction. That may strike you as an odd definition, but I think it's a defensible one. Scholarship is, of course, about research and sessions of sweet, silent thought. But a life of thinking is incomplete unless all that cerebration is turned into something that outlives the moment of its creation.

Perhaps you will become a great teacher. But you can certainly become that professional writer. If you revise your dissertation into a book manuscript and get it accepted for publication you will have cleared one of the steepest hurdles in a young scholar's career. Yet even if you can't get it placed, or if you decide to mine the dissertation for articles and pass directly on to your next big idea, you are becoming a professional writer. Let me place equal stress on those three words—*becoming, professional, writer.* It's only a start, and it's part of a process. It's the first time you will be writing as a bona fide member of the intelligentsia (a membership conferred by your new doctoral degree). You can now claim to be part of the discipline whose great thinkers lured you into their tribe years ago. You are writing, which is what writers do to get their ideas out into the world and the only way they know that they are, after all, writers.

It's unlikely anyone spent much time advising you on your writing while you were toiling away at your dissertation. More time was probably spent on your choice of topic and materials, the shape of the argument, or the way in which your thesis might work strategically in relation to disciplinary politics or developing trends. If you revise merely to get your book published, and succeed in doing so, that's fine. But I urge you to take the bigger view: think of the task of revising the dissertation as an exercise in relearning how to write, that is, how to think with words as a tool of expression and communication. Many scholarly authors are happy to use language to convey the complexity of their thoughts, but trying too hard to express, or impress, can result in prose that is unnecessarily difficult to read. Books of this kind aren't much read except by those who must. The rare scholar who can transcend this academic cliché wants to be heard, and will be. He writes as if he believes that the act of communication is crucial to his work.

Listening to one's own prose, shaping one's work for real readers, giving care to openings and closings, attending to the throughline of your manuscript, disciplining your footnotes, holding the voices of supporting scholars in proper balance, all these tricks (though not one of them is tricky or a secret) will make you a better writer. And strangely, a better writer becomes a better thinker.

Who isn't tired of hearing the same laments about the publish-or-perish climate of the modern university? Whenever these conversations get going I wait to see how long it will be before some party's cynicism will be deplored: the university's, for demanding that scholars publish books "no one will read—least of all the administrators"; the publisher's, for selecting "books that will sell" (as opposed, presumably, to whatever the speaker herself is working on); the academic's, for choosing topics that presumably advance a career instead of truth and beauty. It is clear that twenty-first-century scholars are expected to write and to publish, and to do much more of either than did their colleagues a generation ago. You may be hired at a school where three articles were enough for tenure thirty years ago; today, by contrast, two well-reviewed books in seven years will put you in the running for a similar position. That's the world into which you now step.

Let me make a plea for a noncynical view. Scholars who write and publish are probably happier than those who don't. This is a completely impressionistic take, I admit, and there are doubtless deeply depressed academics who nonetheless publish furiously. But like physical exercise, writing is the tiring thing that gives you more energy after you've done it. Writing is a risk, and risk is exciting, and excitement is something you will fight to sustain in your professional life as you age and your students don't.

Becoming a professional writer of nonfiction can be much broader than the traditional academic career path, too. As you move up and out from the dissertation book to the next and the one after that, look for opportunities to write for other kinds of audiences. There is a world of writing opportunities for a fertile mind, even as the academic in search of those opportunities will need to retool his assumptions about audience and form. You may be able to communicate some of the excitement of your discipline's investigations and arguments to a wider community through magazine or newspaper writing, even as you pursue the specialized work that is at the heart of your scholarly career. Basic (but mind-expanding) introductions can be written for the student who will never pursue your field beyond the 100-level course. There are ideas to be disseminated through other media—online, over the radio, at teach-ins. To do that, you will need to write, frequently, daily if you can. The scholar's life is a writing life, and the dissertation is the first piece of it.

In these pages I have tried to lay out tools you can use to turn your doctoral thesis into something others might actually want to read. My perspective is frankly pragmatic, that of an editor and publisher, and what I have to say here reflects my experience at a desk where a lot of dissertations have made a brief appearance. Revision has many faces, of course, and though it is central to any discussion of the doctoral dissertation and what to do with it, it's also a skill that will hold one in good stead throughout one's writing life.

When you have finished your dissertation there is one other document you will revise, and that's your curriculum vitae. There is no pleasure quite as intense and private as the feeling you have when you open the file for your CV and delete the line that says you are an A.B.D. Let your fingers pause over the keyboard. Aim finger at backspace. Delete slowly. Watch those letters chugging backwards into oblivion. Now type in the letters Ph.D. and the date awarded. This is your new life.

But in an important way a curriculum vitae shortchanges an academic's accomplishments, even his identity. Though it records the steps of your educational achievement and implies that you are now a professional thinker, those words never appear exactly that way on the page. More important, it gives no inkling that you are now something else: a professional writer.

"Professional writer" is a funny term. It's normally used to describe someone who earns his living from selling what he writes, like a novelist without a faculty appointment in a writing division somewhere, or a freelance journalist, selling his prose three thousand words at a time. Most of these professional writers haven't passed through the guild-like mysteries of graduate training and emerged, like Tamino and Pamina, from the trials of water and fire. Having survived the culls, the new Ph.D. likely thinks of himself as a scholar *tout court.* How refreshing it would be if, at the end of a dissertation defense, the chair of the committee were to turn to the candidate and say "Congratulations, Dr. Smith, you are now an official scholar, researcher, and *professional writer.* We await the books you have ahead of you." Because that is exactly what a new Ph.D. has become, a full-blown professional writer, a scholar trained in a specialty to which she may now devote her career.

Unless she has decided to take another road entirely, the new Ph.D. can anticipate a lifelong engagement with words and ideas. Even if her work is statistically driven, even if she is a brilliant demographer or econometrician and thriving in a universe of regression analyses and polynomials, her ideas can reach their audience only through the mediation of language. She might use fewer words than someone who is devoting a career to a multivolume history of slavery in Asia, but at a fundamental level this is only a distinction of degree. Thinking isn't enough. The point of being a scholar is not only to discover but to make discoveries known.

Begin revising your dissertation and you are embarking on a career as a writing professional. At this early stage it isn't easy to keep in mind that one of the things tenure brings to many scholars is the opportunity to write on subjects that are broader, more curious, less "academic" than anything one might propose as a dissertation topic or even as a second book written before tenure. For the professional writer within every scholar, tenure offers the freedom to think and write outside the confines of your field's imaginary geography, or conversely to devote yourself to writing about something intensely specialized yet meaningful to you.

Once you have tenure, you might carry on writing more books very much like the one or two you wrote before you achieved a permanent faculty position. But you might also do other things: a trade book that digests your specialty for a readership that will never set foot in a graduate seminar room, a textbook to revitalize a fusty curriculum, even something utterly unacademic like a travel journal or a self-help book. (Then there are fiction and poetry, which it seems are never far from any writer's pen.) All of these can come from the same writing mind. Yours. In fact, everything you write for the rest of your life becomes part of a writing career, twinned with your career as a researcher and teacher and yet eerily independent, too. How many scholars do you know only by the list of their works or even what you've heard about those works? As Auden said of Yeats in his elegy on the Irish poet's death, he became his admirers. A scholar becomes her students, and to an even broader extent her readers. If you haven't heard someone lecture, all that remains is the page, or the online record, and maybe audio or photographic recollections. Of these the written work is surely the most important. So with your own work, and so with all of us.

Think, then, of your dissertation as a very grown-up first step. If you discover that it was a step in the wrong direction you will adjust your coordinates, but you will move forward all the same. If you pull it apart and find only a handful of pieces— very good pieces—among the disarray, make them do their public work. Put them into print. Then move forward. And if you find that your dissertation manuscript has the core of something better within it? Clear your desk, pull out your calendar, grab pens and paper, recharge your laptop, and get going.

Writing is a lifelong occupation, an avocation, a battle, and in it we find out what we think and who we are. Learn to practice the habit of writing. Set aside daily writing time and make the lined pad or the desktop screen your regular companion. Let it become your devotional exercise, even if it is the only devotional practice in your life. Your career as an employed scholar depends on it, though I think the rewards—for you, for the rest of us—are more important even than that. What you write is a part of who you are, and in that sense every volume of your writing is a piece of autobiography. It could be a study of Meissen porcelain manufacture or a book on the geology of Manhattan schist. There might be scores of books on those little figurines or those great slabs of rock, but every single one could only have been written by its own author. A book is a part of that author's restless curiosity about the world.

When you write and keep the work to yourself, you hoard your valuables. But when you write and publish, you share, and you lose nothing in the process. Revising is a way of making writing fit for survival in a competitive commercial environment. It's also a way of thinking with increasing clarity, of taking your ideas and polishing them as you struggle to find the right word, the right shape, the right example. Maybe it's my own quirky take on writing, but it seems to me that clarity, and not just finding the right solution, is the goal most writers most prize.

If he hadn't said them, Goethe's final words—"More light! More light!"—could have been provided for him by a Hollywood scriptwriter. Revision is the act of bringing light, and more of it, into one's writing, and so into one's thought and its representation on the page. Books that are well written enjoy the imitation of immortality we call being read. Revising is the way we move the sentence, the paragraph, the page along, more clearly, more strongly, so we can go back to the first creation—the writing—of yet one more sentence, one more paragraph, one more page. As you revise your dissertation you will turn it into something stronger, clearer, and perhaps along the way into something smarter. This is what writing scholars do. Writing and revising, systole and diastole, are the paired beats of a scholar's life.

Checklist 1: Dissertation vs. Book

Dissertation	Book
• Fulfills an academic requirement	• Fulfills a desire to speak broadly
• Audience: one's dissertation committee	• Audience: thousands of people you don't know
• Rehearses scholarship in the field	• Has absorbed scholarship in the field, and builds on it
• Length: unlimited	• Length: strategically controlled for marketability
• Dependent on quotations, often in blocks	• Quotes others judiciously
• Hides the authorial voice	• Creates and sustains an authorial voice
• Structure demonstrates analytic skills	• Structure demonstrates the throughline
• Examples are numerous, repetitive	• Examples are well chosen and move the story forward
• Few, long chapters	• Several chapters of readable length
• Stops	• Concludes

Checklist 2: Things Not To Do

1. Never assume that even an award-winning dissertation is already a scholarly book.

2. Never assume that a publisher or a reader will treat a first book as a practice exercise.

3. Never submit a manuscript to more than one house at the same time unless you have received each house's consent to a multiple submission.

4. Never conceal from a potential publisher arrangements you have already made for the publication of chapters in journals or in edited volumes.

5. Never send a manuscript to a publisher unless you have been asked to do so.

6. Never assume that an award-winning scholarly book couldn't have begun as a dissertation.

Checklist 3: Manuscript Basics

1. Use 8½″ × 11″ white paper.

2. Put your name, address, and contact information (telephone, e-mail) on the first page.

3. Double-space throughout, including notes, epigraphs, and block quotations. No exceptions.

4. Use good margins—top, bottom, sides.

5. Number the pages of the manuscript consecutively from beginning to end. Do not start at page 1 for each new chapter.

6. Print on one side of the page.

7. Be sure that all charts, diagrams, maps, and illustrations are clearly printed or provided in viewable photocopies. Do not send original art.

8. Save the entire manuscript onto a disk. Create a "Read Me" file and save that to the disk as well. "Read Me" can contain whatever you want to tell your reader about the other files.

9. Plan on sending your publisher two complete hard copies of the manuscript, along with an electronic file. All three must be identical, down to the last keystroke.

10. Package the manuscript securely together with a cover letter. Mail the package to the specific individual who has requested your work.

There are a number of books that can help you write a dissertation. The best ones on the subject focus on the psychological and organizational stumbling blocks every graduate student can recognize. Several pay particular attention to the role of revision in writing the dissertation, how best to take advice from one's director and committee, how to translate that advice into practical terms, how to make the next version of a chapter clearer, sharper, and more to the point. Eviatar Zerubavel's *The Clockwork Muse* (Cambridge: Harvard University Press, 1999) will make you sit up straight, check your watch, and get going. Joan Bolker's *Writing Your Dissertation in Fifteen Minutes a Day* (New York: Henry Holt, 1998) depends on your doing just that, and shows you how you can reach your goal with even a small commitment as long as it is executed religiously. In the view of these aids, the final revision is the one meant to take the dissertation writer all the way to the finish line. You may not break the tape, but you cross on your own two legs. There are other books on how to get the dissertation written. Any book that helps you get through is worth the time you spend reading it.

Of course, there are countless books on how to write. Two widely read ones are William Zinsser's *On Writing Well* (New York: Harper, 1976, reissued 2001) and Anne Lamott's *Bird by Bird* (New York: Anchor, 1995). I also like Betsy Lerner's *The Forest for the Trees* (New York: Riverhead, 2000).

Books on how to get published tend to focus on fiction, and so they generally warn that the route from manuscript to publisher requires an agent. (Most scholarly writers turning a dissertation into a book won't need an agent, and will waste time pursuing one.) A few books on publishing do address the interests and needs of scholarly writers. Trade nonfiction isn't the main concern of *From Dissertation to Book,* but it is the focus of *Thinking Like Your Editor* (New York: Norton, 2002) by publishing veteran Susan Rabiner and Alfred Fortunato. Beth Luey's *Handbook for Academic Authors* (Cambridge: Cambridge University Press, 2002), now in its fourth edition, provides useful information on a range of publishing issues and includes an excellent bibliography. My *Getting It Published* (Chicago: University of Chicago Press, 2001) has a few pages on revising dissertations, and summarizes the other things you need to know if you want to have a book published by an academic publisher. Revising prose is a more elusive subject, and the shelves offer fewer book-length resources. Richard Lanham's *Revising Prose* (Boston: Allyn & Bacon, 1999), now in its fourth edition, is a small and expensive paperback that offers the reader a rigorous program and promises results. For help with the author's last responsibility see Nancy C. Mulvany's *Indexing Books* (Chicago: University of Chicago Press, 1994).

As to revising dissertations, readers in search of something on the subject long turned to *The Thesis and the Book,* published in 1976 by the University of Toronto Press. This brief volume, edited by Eleanor Harman and Ian Montagnes, consists of selected essays from the journal *Scholarly Publishing.* The best pieces in that volume have been retained for the recently published revision, *The Thesis and the Book: A Guide for First-Time Academic Authors* (Toronto: The University of Toronto Press, 2003), edited by Harman, Montagnes, Siobhan McMenemy, and Chris Bucci. Much of what you will find in the new *Thesis and the Book* was written thirty years ago, but it remains of use; the essay by Olive Holmes remains valuable reading.

Most recently, Beth Luey has edited *Revising Your Dissertation: Advice from Leading Editors* (Berkeley: The University of California Press, 2004), which contains new essays by scholarly publishers and editors on topics specific and general. Many voices, but lots of good advice here.

Beyond your "for further reading" list there are the genuinely essential tools you need as a professional scholarly writer. Nothing beats having a good dictionary. (Having several is even better, including a foreign language dictionary or two for the languages that most often find their way into your work.) A good style manual comes next. The *Chicago Manual of Style* is the best. A third must-have, though less well known, is the *AAUP Directory* (New York: Association of American University Presses, 2003). Regularly updated, and published in paperback, the *AAUP Directory* describes scores of university presses (including some outside the United States) and other not-for-profit publishers, providing contact names and numbers as well as information on each press's program. Keep in mind that the *Directory* does not include commercial publishers.

You're a professional now. These titles are your professional aids. Don't just keep them handy, keep them visible. Wear them out with use.

INDEX

advisors: 4, 7; informal, 16
A4 paper, 60
American Sociological Review, 40
Andersen, Hans Christian, 52
APA Stylesheet, 108
Aristotle, 107
articles: publishing chapters as, 39,
    40, 41–42, 72, 123, 128; vs. book,
    24, 25, 26, 28
"as is" submissions, 42
Astaire, Fred, 74
Auden, W. H., 27, 127–28
audience, need to reach, 7, 14, 52,
    58–59, 79, 94, 101
Auerbach, Nina, 85

Bakhtin, Mikhail, 107
Benjamin, Walter, 107
Bhabha, Homi, 15
Bishop, Elizabeth, 36, 37
blind submissions, 31
block quotations, 23, 68, 110
bookstores: 3; Barnes & Noble, 101
boredom, 16
Bourdieu, Pierre, 18
Butler, Judith, 15

careers, changing, 40, 47
chapter notes, 108
Chicago Manual of Style, 108
chronology. *See* structure
citation, excess, 107
clarity, 2, 8, 23, 79, 103, 129
closure, 74
collective reader, imaginary, 105
colons, 77, 115–17
conventions, academic, 57

conclusions, 23, 34, 44, 71, 72, 73–74
contract, 50
cover letter, 54
curriculum vitae, 85, 122–29

deadlines, 67
density, 8, 76
Derrida, Jacques, 18
disappointment, new author's, 2
discomfort, necessary, 9
dissertation: award-winning, 4, 43,
    51; contradictory goals of,
    25–26; as crossroads, 38; decision
    not to revise, 16; defense of,
    1, 10; as dress rehearsal, 7; estab-
    lishing credibility by means
    of, 25; incompleteness of, 44; as
    middle of journey, 17; as not-yet-
    a-book, 15–17; options in revis-
    ing, 4, 38–50; piecemeal growth
    of, 81; plasticity of, 6; publish-
    able, 10; published in series, 42;
    revised, 55; "revised" vs. "un-
    revised," 10, 76; simple formula
    of, 13; too many, 4, 51; unpublish-
    able, 17; unrevisable, 9, 37; unre-
    vised, 13, 42, 43, 107; weaknesses
    in, 60; written as books, 25, 26
dissertation abstract, 87
dissertation committee: 12, 14, 15,
    34, 49, 68, 69, 85, 86, 93; con-
    cerns of, 7, 8
dissertation director, 16, 20–21
dissertation proposal, 12
"dissertation style," 101–4
double-sided copying, 60
Duneier, Mitch, 4

139